From Surviving to Thriving

SUNY Series, The Psychology of Women,

Michele A. Paludi, Editor

From Surviving to Thriving

INCEST, FEMINISM, AND RECOVERY

CHRISTINE DINSMORE

State University of New York Press

Published by
State University of New York Press, Albany

For information, address State University of New York
Press, State University Plaza, Albany, N.Y. 12246

Production by Dana Foote
Marketing by Theresa A. Swierzowski

Library of Congress Cataloging-in-Publication Data

Dinsmore, Christine, 1950–
    From Surviving to Thriving: Incest, Feminism, and Recovery /
Christine Dinsmore.
        p.   cm.—(SUNY series, The psychology of women)
    Includes bibliographical references and index.
    ISBN 0–7914-0628–8 (alk. paper) .—ISBN 0–7914-0629–6 (pbk. :
alk. paper)
        1. Incest victims—Mental health. 2. Women—Mental health.
3. Feminism. 4. Psychotherapy.   I. Title. II. Series.
RC560.I53D56   1991
616.85'83—dc20   90–40378
                                                                              CIP

10 9 8 7 6 5 4 3 2 1

To My Parents,
Ann and Jim Dinsmore

CONTENTS

Contents

viii

FOREWORD

It is a great pleasure to introduce readers to a book about women's bravery, strength, and ultimate triumph over extreme trauma. Over the last twenty years I have worked as a psychotherapist with women struggling to overcome shame, guilt, anxiety, and depression resulting from circumstances imposed by the family and society. In my clinical practice, time and again a woman's problem can often be traced to an earlier trauma of sexual abuse. I am grateful to Christine Dinsmore for writing *From Surviving to Thriving: Incest, Feminism, and Recovery*. In this book, Dinsmore clearly describes how women survivors of incest and sexual abuse can move through various stages of recovery to a point of empowerment where they can thrive in their lives and not merely exist.

In the last few years there have been many fine books written about the trauma of incest. The voices of survivors cry out in pain, rage, and sadness from those pages. However, there has been a critical need for a book focused on the recovery process and written from a feminist perspective. What are the skills that a survivor of incest develops? How can these skills be made useful in adult life? Are there stages of recovery a survivor must navigate? How can a therapist, friend, lover, spouse, or even a child be helpful during the recovery process? As an adult, what kind of relationship might the survivor establish with her mother and/or her father? All of these questions and concerns are considered in *From Surviving to Thriving: Incest, Feminism, and Recovery*.

As Dinsmore explains, it is often meaningless and always destructive to think in terms of degrees of abuse, depending on the manner in which the perpetrator violated the victim. Whether the perpetrator was seductively kind or cruelly sadistic is not the central issue; all sexual abuse is damaging to women regardless of the form it takes. Dinsmore writes that incest is never attributable to a "personal flaw" in the child, but is rather a consequence of the vulnerability and powerlessness of children. She delineates the way young girls develop skills that enable them to survive the abuse. These skills, Dinsmore shows us, are not pathological, but are human responses to an abnormal circumstance. This tenet is brilliantly developed, and it forms the basis of Dinsmore's highly professional and extremely caring work with survivors.

Christine Dinsmore has dedicated herself to working with women who have been both physically and mentally brutalized as children. This book will be of great value to any survivor of incest. Equally important, she teaches the rest of us—therapists, family members, and friends—how to be helpful to the survivor who bravely takes on the task of ending the secrecy, recovering memories, and experiencing feelings. Dinsmore points out that the recovery process is unique for each survivor. You won't find any pat formulas here. Instead, the reader is left with a sensitivity and an awareness of the role one might play in the survivor's journey as she recaptures the life once stolen from her.

Jane R. Hirschmann, C.S.W.
Co-author of *Overcoming Overeating*
and *Solving Your Child's Eating Problems*

PREFACE

*I think that it's useful for people to know these kinds
of things, and I have a personal investment in it
because I feel somehow like terminal cancer patients
when they are told, 'Well you have two months to
live, considering what has happened to you,' and
they go on to live for years and years. And I think
that I am an argument against categorizing people
based on the severity of the abuse.*

These words were spoken by Barbara, age thirty, an Ivy League
Ph.D., who was sadistically tortured and raped by her father from
about age three until he impregnated her at age thirteen. Barbara,
like the other courageous women who will be heard from in the following pages, has actively worked on recovering from the trauma of
childhood sexual abuse.

I met Barbara several years ago when she agreed to be interviewed
for my research on incest recovery. Her words and the words of many
other survivors tell a story of pain and of triumph. Although I have
given identifying information such as age or occupation when a survivor's words are first recorded in these pages, I have changed all
names and I have not attempted to make any one person particularly
identifiable. This is not only their story. This is about all women's
experiences.

Much has been said about incest survivors' being "scarred for life,"
as if that were synonymous with hopelessness and an inability to recover. Fortunately, survivors and their support networks have realized that
those very scars have helped incest victims to become incest survivors.

This book is about the journey from victim to survivor to beyond.
For the sake of this project, *incest* is defined as the sexual seduction,
molestation, and/or rape of a child by an older relative or trusted
friend of the family, including teachers, neighbors, doctors, coaches,
and so on. The term *survivor* is used here to refer to the adult woman
who was sexually victimized as a child. The term *victim* is used to identify the child who is being sexually abused.

The perpetrator is referred to as "he." This is because the sexual abusers of children are overwhelmingly male and because, given the dynamics of power and sexuality in a patriarchal culture, the danger posed to children comes from men. There are women who sexually abuse children, and these children are equally as traumatized as children who are abused by men. All sexual abuse is traumatic. And although most sexual abuse is committed by men, it is not my intention to dismiss the pain of women who were abused by women. In my work with survivors, I have found that the recovery process, for the most part, is the same.

This project began as a doctoral dissertation and grew to be a larger commitment to the survivors who gave me the privilege of learning about their lives. My work with incest survivors, coupled with my research, has allowed this project to evolve. Many of the survivors encouraged this work and actively shared their stories and beliefs as a way of making their incest recovery process a gift to other survivors. This book is my gift to them.

ACKNOWLEDGMENTS

My connection to strong, nurturing women has allowed me to heal from life's battles and continue to grow in spite of obstacles that might have been placed in my path. On a personal level I have learned first-hand how important my connections are. Through this personal knowledge I have been able to be a resource for my clients, and through my connections I have learned that one heals and grows within communities—communities of friends, family, colleagues, and peers. It is because of others that I am who I am. I would like to thank the people who have contributed to my development and to the creation of this book.

As with all works, this book exists because other works came before it. This project stands on the shoulders of numerous books, periodicals, research studies. I am also indebted to professionals working with survivors, and most importantly, incest survivors. My work with incest survivors has been especially influenced by the works of Judith Herman and Sandra Butler—professionals who combined their therapeutic skill with their feminist understanding. Additionally, I wish to thank other mental health professionals who have helped shape my work: Pam Atkins, Jerry Arndt, Horace Belton, Hal Miller, Patricia Mitchell, Ruth Levine, Nancy Rosen, Harold Russell, and Janice Tucci.

I also thank my support network, the women in my life who have encouraged and supported me during the writing of this book: Robbi Bjerum, Beverly Brumm, Pat Clarke, Liza Cowan, Rhonda Crouse, Joan Dikowitz, Alix Dobkin, Jane Hirschmann, Barbara Jackson, Nora Levine, Jill Lippoff, Rebecca McCauley, Tina Moore, Pam Parker, Linda Puglia, and Vera Robinson.

Thanks to Bonnie Gintis and Ellen Sribnick for their gentle, healing touch when my shoulder would go into spasm after long hours in front of my computer.

I thank my parents, Ann and Jim Dinsmore, and my siblings, Jim Dinsmore, Richard Dinsmore, and Ann Marie Brown, and my nephews, Tom and Dan Brown, for their love, support, and understanding.

Additionally I wish to acknowledge the guidance and dedication of my doctoral committee at The Union Institute, who helped shape my original research in the area of incest recovery: Rita Arditti, Patricia Dick, Jean Griffin, Amy Kesselman, Margaret Nichols, and John Schoonbeck.

Thanks to my clients and to the incest survivors who participated in my original research. Their courage and strength helped shape this book.

Thanks to Lois Patton, editor-in-chief at SUNY Press, for her interest in this book when it was just an idea expressed as an outline. Thanks also to Dana Foote, production editor, and Wendy Nelson, copy editor, who carefully attended to the details of this book.

Thanks to Ruth Levine for her love, support, understanding, and nurturance during this and other projects that have kept me always busy and sometimes crazy.

I extend a special thanks to Linda Atkinson, who encouraged me, motivated me, and spent hours with me as I struggled over each word, sentence, and paragraph. She helped get this project started by giving me direction after my years of talking about writing a book on incest recovery. Her critical eye, her commitment to feminist ideals, and her editorial skills were invaluable to me during the writing of this book. Additionally I thank Sara Atkinson, who without complaint shared her mother with me.

CHAPTER ONE

Introduction

This is a book about incest recovery. This is a book about girl victims and women survivors, powerlessness and power, despair and hope, and growing up female in the United States. This is a book about being scarred for life but not damaged beyond repair.

As I wrote this book, I was aware that I have been influenced by many people—my clients in my private psychotherapy practice, professionals in the field, friends and family, and participants in my doctoral research on incest recovery. It's difficult to distinguish my original thoughts on incest recovery from the beliefs I have acquired from others. But then again, is there such a thing as "original thought"? In any event, this is an account of the evolution of my beliefs on incest recovery.

I became knowingly involved with incest survivors ten years ago when I worked with juvenile delinquent girls in a residential treatment agency. I couldn't help but notice that most of the girls sent away by Family Court had some history of sexual abuse. In particular, there seemed to be a high correlation between sexual abuse and the juvenile offenses of prostitution, running away from home, drug-related crimes, and truancy. I decided to look closer at this, and included questions about sexual contact between the child and a relative and the child and an adult as part of the intake process. I discovered that 90 percent of my female clients admitted to some sexual involvement with an adult—often a family member. Ninety percent may seem high; however, I was involved with a population of clients who came to Family Court with serious family problems. Although I believe that my 90 percent may be high, I also believe that Diana Russell's (1982) figure of 38 percent of girls being sexually abused by an adult before the age of eighteen is low.

Regardless of the exact figure, my work with court-adjudicated girls made me realize that the courts may very well have been sending the wrong persons away to be rehabilitated. At that time, I decided to actively address the issues of sexual abuse in these children's lives. Through my work with sexually abused teenage girls I learned concretely what I had known intuitively—men are generally the perpetrators and girls and women are generally the victims of sexual abuse.

As I began talking about what I was noticing among my female clients in treatment, more and more women opened up to me about their own histories of childhood sexual abuse. I began to examine my own childhood and realized what I had viewed as predictable encounters with men were in fact sexual abuse. I began to understand how gender roles were conditioning girls to become victims and boys to become perpetrators. I also realized, much later, however, that talking about incest and childhood sexual abuse without talking about patriarchy and gender roles was not addressing the real causes, and in fact was like putting a band-aid on a hemorrhage. We may have been stopping the individual bleeding, but we were not stopping the onslaught.

To understand that the cause of sexual violence, including incest and other childhood sexual abuse, lies at the doorstep of patriarchy, we need to look at the statistics. Diana Russell (1982) learned from her research the following: 44 percent of women are victims of rape or attempted rape, one out of four women are battered in their primary relationships, one out of seven women are victims of marital rape, 38 percent of all women are sexually abused by an adult before the age of eighteen. These statistics may look shockingly high, but a close look at the research indicates that this may very well be the tip of the iceberg. For instance, in Russell's research methodology, the probability sample, women to be interviewed, were located through the telephone book; this excluded from the sample, from the start, women who were not listed in the phone book—women who were in battered women's shelters, or prisons, or drug or alcohol rehab, or psychiatric hospitals, or homeless shelters, or women who were too poor to have phones. There were women who were missed—many of them at high risk for sexual violence.

In viewing this issue from another angle, Neil Malamuth (1981) interviewed college men and discovered that 51 percent of those interviewed said they would rape a woman if they were sure they would get away with it. I remember my shock when I first read this study and discussed it with a colleague. He laughed at what he called my naiveté, saying, "You can't possibly believe that to be the reality, because you know how adolescent males are—they like to brag about their conquests." I somehow couldn't be comforted by his assurances because they spoke of how boys are conditioned in this society; they are reinforced for sexual violence and their belief in their own sexual entitlement.

What was even more disheartening than the statistics was the fact that behind those statistics were people. As my work with survivors evolved through the years, as I began to work with adult women incest survivors through individual and group therapy, as I began to work with children who were referred to me because of their incest histories, these statistics began to have names and faces. These statistics were my clients, my friends, my family. These statistics were in fact all women, in that each of us is confronted with the reality that we are vulnerable to sexual assault.

We, as women, have a different experience than men. We are taught early that we risk physical harm if we "get out of line," and we in fact risk physical harm even when we are "towing the line." At her presentations on sexual violence, Judith Herman, M.D., often asks the audience (usually predominately female) to raise their hands if they have experienced the following: an obscene phone call, an encounter with an exhibitionist, an encounter with a masher. As the hands go up in the audience, there is usually uncomfortable laughter. Herman then goes on to explain that although the audience is laughing now, they were not laughing when it happened, that these "minor" sexual encounters are very frightening when they are happening. These "minor" sexual encounters serve a purpose in teaching women to know their place. In her *Work in Progress* (1984), Herman states: "Further, in the war between the sexes, I submit that these minor assaults are equivalent to cross burnings or to the discovery of a swastika painted on a building. They are ominous warnings of threats that we prefer to repress, the ultimate threat being the rape-murder. Taken together, the research findings and our gut-level feelings point to a conclusion that no girl or woman is currently safe from sexual assault, and to be female is to be subject to the possibility of a sexual assault."

In working with incest survivors, I have not only learned of the effects of this childhood trauma, I have also learned of women's strengths. The journey that began with my attempt to understand the trauma of childhood sexual abuse that my adolescent clients reported continued as I worked with adult women incest survivors and learned of their strengths. Through this journey, I was influenced by Judith Herman, author also of *Father-Daughter Incest*, and Sandra Butler, author of *Conspiracy of Silence*. Their written work and their presentations helped me to begin to formulate a therapy that would help clients to heal from this trauma. In addition, the women who participated in my doctoral study on incest recovery helped to mold my work. Through my involvement with incest survivors I have learned of the strengths of survivors of childhood sexual assault, and I have learned through them that, yes, they are scarred for life, but they are not damaged beyond repair. We must focus on their strengths to enhance the recovery process. We must celebrate the scars and honor the survival skills that helped the child make it through her childhood.

I remember once being told of a "scientific" phenomenon that was illustrated in a story by Ken Keyes (1981). There is a group of islands off Japan where monkeys live, each island isolated from the others. On one of the islands, one monkey decided to wash its yam in the water before eating it. (S)he did that every day, and soon other monkeys on the island began washing their yams in the water before eating them. In time, all the monkeys on that island were washing their yams before eating them. Somehow, when the hundredth monkey began washing its yams, not only were all the monkeys on that island washing theirs, but the monkeys on all the other islands were washing their yams as well. This story was offered as an example of how one's action can change the course of events without any concrete interaction among individuals, that one becomes two, becomes four, and so on, ad infinitum. This story may or may not be true. However, I believe that the same dynamic exists today with women. In 1988, I stated in my doctoral dissertation that I had decided to research the area of incest recovery because there was little information on the subject. There was an enormous amount of literature on the trauma of incest but little on healing. In just the past two years, more has been published on incest recovery. It seems as if there were people throughout the United States, unbeknownst to each other, who began to research the question, Does one recover from the trauma of incest? Like the example of the monkeys and the yams, women are creating a collective energy to focus on the trauma of childhood sexual abuse and to empower themselves as survivors. And women are going beyond being survivors to become thrivers. We are changing our lives and the lives of the generations to follow. This book is about that process.

CHAPTER TWO

Feminist Therapy

Feminist therapy is about change: it is concerned with the process as well as the outcome, a process that is political yet grounded in women's personal experiences. It holds the belief that the personal and the political are very much connected. As a feminist therapist, I see the sexual abuse history of a woman client not only as her personal history but also as it relates to the larger picture of violence against women in our culture. How we, as women, have been socialized to become victims and how men have been socialized to be aggressors are understood. The feminist therapy process is respectful of women's strengths and recognizes women to be the experts on their conditions. Therefore the feminist therapist is not set up to be the authority but rather is the facilitator. It is my job as a feminist therapist to bear witness. I often tell my clients that they are doing the work. I'm the cheerleader.

Feminist therapy sees women as an oppressed group. As feminist therapists, we look at the *interpersonal* issues, such as relational dynamics, as well as the *intrapsychic* issues, emotional responses, that our clients bring to therapy. We recognize the political and social context of what it means to be a woman in this culture. Unlike other therapies, feminist therapy is a means of empowering women rather than helping them adjust to the status quo.

In addition to looking at gender issues, feminist therapy examines issues of race, class, age, and sexual orientation. For instance, if my client is an African-American lesbian incest survivor, I am aware that in addition to what she has internalized because of her incest history, she may be feeling self-hatred as a member of an oppressed minority; she may have internalized the racism and homophobia of our culture, which will further complicate her incest recovery process. Since incest survivors, because of their childhood traumas, generally feel different from the rest of the world, I will be certain not to include only one

African-American woman or one lesbian or one Asian woman in an incest survivors' group. As a feminist therapist, I am aware of issues of racism, classism, ageism, and heterosexism and how they further compound one's feeling different from the rest of the world. The political knowledge of these issues directly impacts on the work I do.

Feminist therapy also understands that certain behaviors result not from pathology but rather from conditioning. For instance, women have been taught to enable, within relationships. In learning gender roles, they learn to put their needs behind those of others—partners, children, friends—yet this behavior gets translated in traditional therapy as co-dependency. In feminist therapy, the therapist helps the client look at the times when her desire to nurture relationships exists at the expense of her own needs.

Feminist therapy is not a technique but rather a process. One can be a gestalt therapist, a jungian therapist, a bioenergetics therapist, an eclectic therapist, and so on, and still be a feminist therapist. It is the recognition of women as an oppressed group and the goal of helping women to make changes for themselves and their environment, rather than specific schools, interventions, or skills, that are the backbone of feminist therapy.

Feminism is my orientation. As a therapist, however, I have an obligation not to have my feminist values get in the way of the client's process. The beliefs and values I bring to my work help me honor women's strengths and respect their histories, and my work as a feminist therapist allows me to understand that women's words and experiences have not been valued by our culture and that women have internalized the misogynist beliefs that permeate our culture. But it is not my job, as a feminist therapist, to impose my values and beliefs on my clients.

When values get in the way, as they can with any orientation, sometimes feminist therapists are too quick to see the incest survivor's mother as a victim. The feminist therapist may want to talk about the mother's position, her powerlessness in an abusive family, rather than allowing the client to rage at her mother for not protecting her. Therapists must honor their clients' stages. Survivors must be allowed to heal in their own ways. Raging at one's mother for allowing the incest to happen and for not protecting her is a necessary step in the survivor's healing process. In time, as the survivor analyzes the family dynamics and begins to see how tyranny was maintained within the family, she may reevaluate the role her mother played in her life. But until that happens, the therapist must keep her politics about mothers to herself.

Sometimes feminist therapists have trouble hearing not only the survivor's anger toward her mother but also her love for her perpetrator. Survivors may have mixed feelings, including loving feelings, toward perpetrators. No one is all bad, and even perpetrators may have wonderful qualities that the survivor recognizes; the survivor may see him as the only one who gave her attention and love. It is important that the therapist not prematurely express her own anger at the perpetrator, for she might cause the survivor to feel guilty for loving him or having loved him. In response to the therapist's anger, the survivor may feel that she was somehow complicitous or that she is evil for loving the man who abused her. Additionally, the survivor may stop talking honestly with the therapist, as she will feel judged and unaccepted. As the therapy unfolds and the recovery process continues, the survivor will evaluate the roles of her mother, father, and siblings and learn to distinguish abuse from love, defenselessness from power, and tyranny from benevolence.

Sometimes feminist therapists have difficulty when their incest survivor clients are sexually aroused by stories of sexual violence. As a feminist, the therapist might get stuck on how "politically incorrect" it seems to be aroused by male sexual violence. However, it is common for incest survivors to become aroused by tales of sexual abuse, and often they feel guilty and ashamed about this. Some may never even mention it. It is important for the feminist therapist to be aware of how common this is and to recognize it as a normal response to an abnormal childhood. It is important, too, that the therapist bring this issue up and give the survivor an opportunity to talk about it, to let her know that being aroused by sexual violence is not uncommon. Therefore it is essential for the feminist therapist to get rid of the notion of political correctness as it pertains to the incest recovery process.

Feminist therapy has feminism at its theoretical base without imposing feminist values on the client. It understands the many aspects of being a woman in this culture. Feminist therapy recognizes that anger has been trivialized for women and acknowledges its importance to the healing process. And feminist therapy, recognizing how women's bodies have been stolen from them and that women are seen as sexual objects, works with women in reclaiming their bodies. Sometimes this means working with other healers (massage, chiropractic, shiatsu, etc.) toward the same goal; sometimes it means helping women learn to enjoy their bodies and may include involvement in sex therapy. Feminist therapy recognizes that the mother–daughter bond has been severed by the patriarchy and works toward addressing mother–daughter issues. Feminist therapy recognizes that women have been cheated out of their history and that they may be lacking in role models—and that the therapist may be the survivor's only role model of a strong, capable woman. Specific ways of working with issues of anger, sex, intimacy, mothers–daughters, reclaiming the body, and so on, are discussed more fully in later chapters.

The feminist therapist has a difficult task. She must embrace feminism as it pertains to being a woman in our society, but she must be careful not to impose these views on her clients. She must be able to refrain from having her issues become her clients' issues. She must allow for the recovery process to unfold without interfering. This may be difficult when the client is experiencing emotions that are counter to what the therapist is feeling, but the client's process is what matters here, not the therapist's. If the therapist finds this too difficult, she should seek clinical supervision. An effective feminist therapist should be able to work with nonfeminists and feminists alike. We do this by respecting and honoring all the women with whom we work, regardless of where they are within the healing continuum.

Feminist therapy recognizes that both women's and men's development are the results of patriarchal conditioning. For instance, it is not surprising that post traumatic stress disorder (PTSD), a common diagnosis for women who were sexually abused and men who were in combat, is manifested differently among women than among men. In women, PTSD often results in self-abusive behavior, whereas in men PTSD often results in aggressive, outward violence. When we talk in feminist terms about the abuse of women, we are talking about the way people are conditioned to function and do function when they are raised in a patriarchal culture. This often results in women being victims and men being abusers.

It is my feminist orientation that has launched this book. For I have seen that in spite of public acknowledgment, increasing visibility, and individuals speaking out about sexual violence, there doesn't seem to be a decrease in the sexual abuse of children, and perhaps there has even been an increase. I believe that part of the reason may be the fact that in all the acknowledgments and literature, naming the violence has been avoided; and I believe that a feminist analysis is necessary, not to blame a segment of the population, but rather to challenge the patriarchal imbalance that causes violence against women and children. It is necessary to make this challenge so that women who have survived sexual assault will understand that the violence they endured was the result not of individual flaws but rather of the politics of being powerless in the culture. This is a way of examining incest and recovery by truly recognizing that the personal and the political are connected.

CHAPTER THREE

Historical Perspective

Incest has existed throughout recorded history. Every society has had an incest taboo, although what determines an act to be incest varies from culture to culture. I define incest as the sexual seduction, molestation, and/or rape of a child by an older relative or trusted friend of the family. By this definition, incest has existed in every human culture of which we have any knowledge.

Florence Rush, in *The Best Kept Secret* (1980), gives a thorough account of the role of the Talmud and the Bible in sanctioning the sexual abuse of children. She notes, for instance, that Talmudic law prohibits betrothal or marriage before the age of three years and one day. Although there is controversy in this area, and other students of the Talmud and the Judaic tradition—for example, Rachel Biale, in *Women and Jewish Law* (1984)—would take issue with Rush's interpretation, the point remains that incest has been part of the human community for as long as we have records. But I do not wish to duplicate the works of others who have investigated Talmudic law and Biblical law, child marriage, child prostitution, and the child pornography industry (Armstrong, 1982; Barry, Bunch, and Castley, 1984; Dworkin, 1974; Rush, 1980); instead I wish to begin this historical journey with Sigmund Freud, for it was Freud, considered the father of modern psychiatry, who began the collective denial of incest. Freud knew the "secret" of childhood sexual abuse but did not have the courage or perhaps the desire to accuse his compatriots. In effect, therefore, it was Freud who may be guilty of the worst betrayal of all.

In 1896, Freud presented a paper called "The Aetiology of Hysteria" (Strachey, 1962), in which he spoke of the sexual abuse of children. He had discovered, he said, that the cause of hysteria, a common diagnosis of Victorian women, was childhood sexual abuse, and the extensive data he presented included numerous case studies of women who had been sexually exploited by the adults who had cared for them.

This paper may initially seem to have been a courageous act by Freud, but its force was diluted by his claim that the sexual abusers were primarily wet nurses and nannies. Was it somehow inconceivable to him that men, particularly fathers, could be involved in such atrocities—or was he just protecting the patriarchal view of the world, as he had done previously and would do in subsequent works? For it has not been only *this* betrayal of women that has warped the view of the psychology of women. It was Freud who again articulated the patriarchal view of women—that women are deficient men—and subsequently gave psychology the vocabulary of penis envy, the Oedipus complex, women's sexual wish/fantasies about their fathers, and so on.

Falsely naming the perpetrator was not Freud's greatest betrayal. As he began to document tales of father–daughter incest and felt the negative responses of his colleagues to this theory, in an astonishing about-face he changed his position. In 1924, Freud added a footnote to his earlier paper on hysteria. He stated that when he had presented his theory in 1896, he had not yet freed himself of "my overvaluation of reality and my low valuation of phantasy" (Strachey, 1962). In essence he was saying that he had been naive when he had believed his clients' reports of childhood sexual abuse and that he now realized that these women had been reporting merely their fantasies, their desires for sexual involvement with adults—primarily, he believed, with their fathers. Thus Freud, who had an opportunity to intervene on behalf of his women clients, instead began the long history of the denial of women's reality. It is important to emphasize this. This denial did not concern only the few women whose stories were dismissed because of it; it was the underscoring of women's position in Victorian society and the societies to follow. Woman was portrayed as being sexually, psychologically, and intellectually immature—a vamp who could not be trusted to distinguish her fantasy from her reality. One small betrayal for his women patients, one giant betrayal for womankind.

Needless to say, because of Freud's historical importance, the denial of this aspect of women's reality has continued to the present day. There are still those who do not believe that children or women are sexually abused in the numbers that are reported, and for this reason crimes such as incest and rape continue to be the hardest crimes to convict. The belief that girls and women desire to be raped resulted in Judge William Reinecke's giving this explanation for his having sentenced to a work-release program a man convicted of sexually assaulting the five-year-old daughter of his paramour: "I am satisfied that we have an unusually sexually promiscuous young lady, and he did not know enough to refuse. No way do I believe the man initiated sexual contact" (Herman, 1984). So an incest perpetrator is given leniency because the judge believes him to be the victim of a seductive five-year-old. After all, how can someone argue with the notion that girls secretly desire to have sex with their fathers, or in this case father substitutes, when the "father of psychiatry" set the precedent with his now-famous fantasy/wish theory. It is not surprising that feminist psychology challenges psychoanalytical thought as developed by Freud.

For almost fifty years following Freud's 1924 paper, there was no public discussion of incest. But in the early 1970s, the women's movement gave rise to consciousness-raising groups in which women began talking to one another about sexual violence. From these groups came the beginning of public discussion of sexual violence against women. In 1971, the first speakout on rape was held in New York City. In 1972, the first rape crisis center was established by the Bay Area Women Against Rape (Herman, 1984). As women began to speak about sexual violence, incest too began to be discussed, and research in this area began to appear. What happened in the process was that women learned that their personal experiences were in fact political, that what they had considered individual events had in fact happened to them not as individuals but as women. Prior to the women's movement and the resulting CR groups, a woman who had been sexually victimized as a child by her father, grandfather, uncle, brother, or other trusted adult, believed that she was the only one who experienced this ultimate violation of trust. As a child who was being manipulated and controlled by the perpetrator (which is discussed more fully in chapter 12), she carried with her to adulthood the "secret." Isolated from other women, she believed that it was some flaw in her character that singled her out to be victimized. The women's movement of the 1970s, by bringing the topic of incest and other forms of sexual violence to the surface, allowed women to realize that as individual women they were not alone.

Although the women's movement ended the silence surrounding sexual violence against women, feminists were not the only ones who tried to explain it. Several views about incest were put forward: Incest is the result of an exaggeration of male norms in our culture (Armstrong, 1982; Herman, 1982, 1984, 1986; Rush, 1980); incest is the result of a dysfunctional family (Armstrong, 1982); incest is the result of pedophiles who are either fixated or regressed (Groth, 1979; Groth & Sgroi, 1986).

Let's begin with the theory that incest is the result of pedophiles who are either fixated or regressed. This idea is based on work with incarcerated men convicted of sexual crimes. Perhaps the most influential proponent of this view is Nicholas Groth, author of *Men Who Rape: The Psychology of the Offender* (1979). In his book, and in other studies and presentations, Groth describes the male pedophile as someone who sexually uses children to gratify his needs for power, love, companionship, and so on. If he is "fixated," he relates to children almost exclusively, as he has an infantile personality and is unable to relate to adults. If he is "regressed," he sexually abuses children when under emotional or psychological stress but usually interacts with age-appropriate companions. A regressed pedophile usually seeks to have his intimacy needs satisfied by an adult but under stress will seek out children, whereas a fixated pedophile almost exclusively satisfies intimacy needs with children. Groth admits that perpetrators do not look psychologically different from nonperpetrators if measured by psychological tests, but he presents a profile of the pedophile that includes having been sexually abused as a child and implies that pedophiles are responsible for incest and other forms of child sexual abuse. Thus he implies that the sexual abuse of children is done by psychologically disturbed men.

There are many problems with this theory, but perhaps the most obvious one is that it is based entirely on a prison population. According to Diana Russell's research (1986), only 6 percent of incest survivors reported the sexual abuse to the police, and only 1 percent resulted in conviction. Therefore, Groth is basing his findings on 1 percent of the perpetrator population—a skewed sample, indeed.

In the final analysis, however, the descriptions of perpetrators given by incest survivors themselves refute the pedophile theory. Survivors consistently use such terms as *pillar of the community, respected breadwinner,* and *the deacon of the church,* when describing the men who abused them. In my own work interviewing incest survivors, I have been told time after time about perpetrators who were highly respected members of their communities. One woman told of having been viciously tortured by her father. He would burn her with cigarettes, stick objects into her rectum and vagina, and walk her on a dog's leash before having her perform oral sex on him. Her father was never imprisoned, never psychiatrically hospitalized, and in fact was a respected businessman in his community. This is not to say that disturbed men do not engage in the sexual abuse of children, but rather that they are not the only ones who do so. In fact, more commonly perpetrators are men who look quite normal.

What about the view that incest is the result of a dysfunctional family? This became a popular theory when society discovered that incest was happening in "good families" as well as "bad families." If incest could not be explained as the work of a few sick men, then what was going on? The family therapists' explanation was that incest was the result of a "family system" gone wrong. What was particularly noticeable about the emergence of this theory was that we began to see such terms as *the complicitous mother; the distant, detached wife; the absent, disabled mother; the frustrated father.* It was implied that mothers were somehow to blame when fathers committed incest, and that fathers were victims who were attempting to meet their needs inappropriately. In addition, since the family therapy approach held the notion that each family member owned a piece of the problem, the incested child, as a member of the "system," also deserved some of the blame. To say that this belief was a disservice to the incest victim/survivor is an understatement.

Although family therapists do not advocate incest and are in fact attempting to intervene in these abusive family systems, there are, as I have mentioned, serious problems with this theory. First and foremost is the victim blaming. Second is the fact that mothers often take the rap for their husbands' or paramours' behavior. This is not to deny that some women are complicitous in incest acts. They know consciously or unconsciously that something is not right in the relationship between the incestuous parties. However, in most cases where she fails to protect her children, the mother is bound to the abuser because he is her economic lifeline, or she too is being abused by him. She cannot protect herself, let alone her children. Not having any economic power or decision-making power, being isolated from others by being relegated to working only in the home, being kept from family and friends, and being physically and psychologically abused does not afford someone the opportunity to protect her children. Mothers are often captives in abusive family systems. This, nonetheless, results in children not being protected from abuse. The job to protect is seen as the role of mothers, so it is understandable that the child-victim and later the adult-survivor is enraged for not having been protected (as discussed in chapter 14).

In a great majority of cases, mothers do not know the abuse is occurring. One woman whose husband sexually abused her oldest daughter worked the night shift at a local hospital. One morning when she arrived home from work, her husband told her that their daughter had told him that she had been raped. He said that the daughter explained that a month earlier, while both parents were away, a man entered their home and raped her; she had been afraid to tell them, but now she was late for her period and she was worried that the rapist had gotten her pregnant. The mother and father raced to the school and took their daughter out of class so that they could report the incident to the police. The mother recalls, "As we were driving to the police station, John [her husband] said to Marsha [her daughter], 'Tell Mommy the story.' Marsha told me how this man came into the house one evening and raped her." At the police station, the police officer asked that the mother and father leave the room while she questioned their daughter. After about twenty minutes, the police officer walked out and she began to read the father his Miranda rights. The truth, of course, was that there was no stranger rape but rather an ongoing incestuous rape of the daughter by the father. Months after the father pleaded guilty in criminal court, the mother explained to me how guilty she felt for not having known about the sexual abuse. "In hindsight I believe I should have known. He was always asking about whether Marsha got her period or if I knew if she was seeing any boys at school. I just always thought it was a father's concern for the well-being of his daughter. Little did I know that he was just checking to make sure that he hadn't gotten her pregnant and that she was exclusively his. Even when I think about it, John saying in the car as we drove to the police station, 'Tell mommy the story.' He actually told her what to tell me in the event that she got pregnant." Marsha may believe that her mother knew of the abuse, but the fact is she didn't. When she found out about the incest, the mother cooperated with the courts so that her husband would be held accountable—she stuck by her daughter even though the family lost their house and car and their economic stability when the father was sent to prison.

Before discussing the feminist view on the causes of incest, I think that it is important to mention that there is a pro-incest lobby that believes that incest is not harmful and that it in fact may be quite beneficial for the child. As reported by Louise Armstrong in her very important article "The Cradle of Sexual Politics: Incest," in *Women's*

Sexual Experiences (1982), the René Guyon Society believes that incest is mutually beneficial to adult and child—that there can be consensual sex between child and adult, and that such sex can be a beautiful, loving experience, an initiation in which the child learns about sex from a caring adult. But the fact is that a child cannot consent to sex with an adult because of the very nature of the power differential, the inherent power an adult possesses over children. Through manipulation, seduction, gifts, praise, and affection, an adult may give the child the impression that she has some choice in the matter; but a child does not have the ability to challenge someone more powerful than she. That is the basis of the statutory rape laws—the belief that children do not have the ability or power to make conscious decisions in sexual matters with adults. More importantly, however, in my years of working with incest survivors I have never had one survivor report to me the benefits she received by being sexually involved with an adult. There may have been secondary gains, such as rewards, attention, and praise, but never has the sexual violation itself been perceived as beneficial.

Incest is the direct result of the male norms in our culture. It is an exaggerated but logical extension of these norms. This is the feminist perspective of the causes of incest. This is my perspective. It does not mean that all men, or even most men, sexually abuse children. But it does acknowledge and hold accountable norms for men that encourage and in fact urge men to be aggressive, dominant, victorious, sexual, and powerful and to see sexual involvement as an entitlement. We only have to recall Neil Malamuth's study, in which 51 percent of college men interviewed said that they would rape a woman if they were sure that they would not get caught—or my colleague's attempt to comfort me by assuring me that those college men wouldn't *really* engage in rape, that they only said that because men like to brag about their sexual conquests.

I think that most women when reflecting on how they were raised will agree that as girls they were taught to put their needs last, to conform to others' expectations, and to be sexually attractive but to save their sexual selves for that one special man. Even today, with all the influence the women's movement has on our society, girls are still given the message that in order to be successful women they must be able to work outside the home, work inside the home, and attract a good man. Our brothers, on the other hand, were taught to achieve, to strive to meet their needs, to be independent, and to have their sexual conquests (as long, of course, as they didn't get the girl pregnant). Even today, although some families are attempting to change how their children are raised, a double standard still exists.

It is with these attitudes and values that girls and boys develop. The norm for a girl is for her needs to be considered secondary to those of others. When she is an adult, that will translate into putting her needs after her partner's and her children's. The norm for a boy is to set his sights on a particular goal and go for it at any cost. When he is an adult, that will translate into believing that the world is his to use and enjoy. Men whose needs don't get met may stoop to other means to achieve some feelings of power. When that happens— women and children beware!

The feminist view, in addition to offering what I believe to be the real explanation of incest, raises important issues regarding women's psychological development. We as women live in fear of sexual assault. We are profoundly affected by the knowledge that we can be victims of sexual violence, and many of us have been victims of sexual violence prior to reaching adulthood. However, we do not talk about this violence. We do not name the violence; we use such terms as *rape victim* and *incest survivor* rather than *rapist, perpetrator,* or *molester.* This subtle linguistic phenomenon powerfully implies that women are the subjects (implying the cause of the action) of male violence rather than the objects. Patriarchy and the resulting male violence are the causes, thus the subjects, of women's victimization. Without explicit discussion about male sexual violence, we as women repress our fears. It is these repressed fears that impact on our development. We internalize our fears and become the subjects of male-dominated psychology, which describes us in such terms as *sexually dysfunctioning, frigid, promiscuous, depressed, eating disordered, overbearing,* and *overprotective.*

Sexual violence and male privilege affects not only women's individual development but also mother–daughter relationships. How often mothers and daughters are in conflict over the unmentionable—the fact that we are potential victims of male violence. The words are not spoken; instead there is conflict over make-up, boyfriends, curfews, hitchhiking, contraceptives, drinking, drugs. What results is a battle between mother and daughter without the real issues being named. Mother the Jailer is seen as the problem, when the real problems are sexual violence and patriarchy. The mother–daughter bond is an untapped source for women's psychological development. Incest severs that bond. The patriarchy severs that bond. Unlike Freud's claiming that we must achieve psychological/ sexual development by mastering the oedipal stage, I believe that women's development will be enhanced with an emphasis on a life-giving mother–daughter bond. This begins with naming male violence of all kinds and confronting the taboo against speaking about sexual violence, including incest.

The history of our ability and willingness to deal with incest is complex, revealing, and heartening. We have moved from outright denial, through theories which posited the pathology of the perpetrator, to those that posited the pathology of the family, to the feminist view that asks us to name the violence and begin to move in a new direction, beyond the place where women are victims and survivors to a place where they are whole.

CHAPTER FOUR

The Incest Trauma

Incest is traumatic. For most people that is probably not a surprising statement. In spite of perpetrators' rationalizations and denials—such claims as "she wanted it" or "better she learn from someone who cares than from a boy on the street" or "she always seemed to enjoy it"—every incest survivor with whom I have spoken has reported incest to be a horrendous experience. Whether the incest was with a father, a brother, an uncle, a grandfather, whether the incest was seductive, gentle, or torturous, whether it happened a few times in a short period of time or it continued for many years, incest has traumatic effects on the girl or woman.

Incest robs children of their childhoods, of their sexual selves, of the basic ingredients for healthy relationships—intimacy, trust, boundaries, security, self-esteem. Incest may take on many different forms—violent and brutal, loving and gentle, a mixture of both violent and gentle; it may result in different responses—sensuous and sexual, fear and terror, powerlessness and loss of self, losses of large blocks of time; but regardless of its form and the child's response, incest is a devastating experience and leaves a devastating mark on its victim.

I recall the words of Patricia, a forty-one-year-old social worker, who explained the effects of the ongoing incestuous relationship she had with her father as a child.

> I was the wife of my father. I was the sexy child. It was a bit of a setup. I was also the battered child. Battered by him. I was the only one that got hit. The battering and the seduction were kind of connected. I was the only child who got thrown against the wall. And then there were great apologies by my father. There were a lot of scenes that seemed very romantic to me. I'd think, 'I'm never going to speak to him

again.' And then he would woo me back. The sexual abuse was physically pleasurable, and it was a way of getting positive attention from my father. But I knew it wasn't right. I had a lot of guilt about it, dread actually. I had physical pleasure of sex, positive attention, and the daringness of a secret. Yet I've always been angry at men. I think that I spent a good number of years being rather promiscuous as a result of trying to conquer men. I think it gives you a guilty notion of your sexuality when your first relationship is illicit. I had a mixed message. I was very proud of my sexuality. I was the sexy one in the family—that was a virtue, a value, a positive—but it was the only thing I thought I had going for me that could get me into a relationship.

Patricia's account exemplifies the conflicting feelings a child may have about a sexual relationship with an adult. In spite of physical pleasure, attention, and other rewards, incest affects the child-victim and the woman-survivor in many negative ways. In particular when sexual pleasure results from the incestuous act, the girl or woman feels betrayed not only by the perpetrator but by her own body as well. Thus, whether Patricia focuses on the battering or on the pleasure and rewards, she still comes up with the same conclusion—incest was a destructive force in her life.

Even when the incest seems relatively benign, survivors report it to have been traumatic. For example, Linda, a twenty-five-year-old student, recalls: "I remember details of separate incidents, but they blur together. He'd always be feeling the sides of my breasts. He considered me a surrogate wife. He'd say, 'If I hadn't married your mother, I'd marry you.' My father says that it started at age nine. It began as tentative [and progressed] to grabbing my breasts. I've never been able to forgive him for that. It was one of the most horrendous experiences of my life."

The violation of the basic trust between father and daughter and the feeling of powerlessness in an unequal relationship are devastating for its victims regardless of the severity of the abuse. Linda has been involved in incest recovery therapy for years, and she is well aware that the sexual abuse she suffered at the hands of her father, mixed though it was with praise and status, has touched every part of her life.

Fathers are not the only men who sexually abuse children. Brothers, uncles, grandfathers, and surrogate family members can also do great damage. When someone is in a position of power or authority, a breaking of boundaries and trust can wreak havoc on a child's perception of herself and her world. When a child is given the message that the older people who know her will love her and protect her, and then instead an older, trusted member of her family abuses her, the child's sense of reality becomes distorted. She begins to doubt her understanding of reality because she is experiencing one thing (sexual abuse) but is told that she is actually experiencing something else (love, care, protection, etc.). This mistrust of her perception often follows her into adulthood. She continues to doubt her perception of the world. This may be manifested in many ways, such as needing to check with others about what she is feeling or experiencing, double- and triple-checking simple tasks such as turning on her alarm clock, and being unable to make decisions for fear that she is not understanding or seeing the whole picture.

As a way of coping with sexual abuse, children develop survival behaviors that help them make it through their childhoods. These survival skills may include dissociation, hypervigilance, isolation, and/or using sex as a negotiating tool. These survival techniques are necessary to help the child-victim survive a pathological adult–child relationship. They are normal responses to abnormal childhoods.

Survival skills acquired in childhood usually continue into adulthood, where some therapists are quick to label them "pathological." I disagree with that label. They are symptoms of incest and need to be addressed, but they are not pathological. These behaviors are learned skills that were necessary for survival. For a woman who is not being sexual or who is being sexual without emotional attachment to simply be labeled "sexually dysfunctional" is a denial of the woman's incest history; when a woman's first sexual encounter was intrusive and traumatic, sex is connected to horrendous memories, and emotional detachment may be necessary. Similarly, for a woman who is bulimic to be labeled as "having an eating disorder" focuses on the symptom rather than the cause; when a child has had a penis forced into her mouth, and as an adult binges on food and regularly vomits, she may be symbolically vomiting out that penis. There is much to be purged. In the same way, a woman who is nervous and attentive to details in her environment would probably be labeled "hypervigilant" by many therapists. But such behavior makes perfect sense if as a child she had to be "on alert" to ward off the sexual intruders in her life. When she is not sure who will be entering her bed at night, she better be attentive; when a certain look in her father's eyes can tell her whether she is in danger tonight or whether she is safe, she better be in tune with the nonverbal cues in her environment. Is it any wonder that as an adult, she continues anxiously to be aware of her surroundings? A woman who does not remember her childhood is called "dissociative." But when a woman's childhood was filled with traumatic sexual assault, is it any wonder that she blocks these horrifying memories? So when therapists look at symptoms and label them "pathology," often they are not addressing the underlying issue—incest. This is what Sandra Butler (1986) calls "parallel denial": the client and therapist examine the symptoms but deny the reality of a history of incest. Instead of identifying incest in the life of the client, they dance around that issue and look only at the "problem behaviors"—hypervigilance, eating disorders, sexual dysfunctions, and so forth. But it is essential to acknowledge and understand these "symptoms" as survival behaviors, for without them there is little possibility for the child-victim to have become the woman-survivor.

In my work with incest survivors, we examine survival behaviors and attempt to determine which of these skills, if any, may in fact still be useful. For instance, a woman who resorts to an old behavior of cutting herself to localize her pain or to punish herself because of the guilt she carries with her may no longer need to do this to work through her emotional agony. If we agree that it's no longer necessary, we work on skills that she can substitute for this once-comforting act. On the other hand, if the survivor is hypervigilant, being highly in tune with her environment, we may recognize that hypervigilance not only served her well in the past but continues to be life-serving behavior in the present, for it is not unwise for us as women to be aware of who's behind us on the street or what noise we might hear from an adjoining room. In other words, we do not assume that all survival skills acquired as the result of an abusive childhood are debilitating and need to be eradicated. Just as children need to learn skills to survive their childhoods, women need to learn skills to survive the patriarchy. Incest survivors need to celebrate their survival skills, examine each one individually, and decide which are no longer necessary and which may continue to be useful.

In honoring survival skills, it is important to look at their origins. In examining these skills as childhood coping mechanisms, we can begin to see the strength and creativity of women survivors, strength and creativity that began long before, when they were girls and victims.

Some forms of dissociative behavior, such as leaving one's body in a way in which the body is present but the conscious mind is subjectively experienced as detached, is quite common. Many women describe their feelings of having watched the incest act from outside their own bodies as if they were watching a movie rather than experiencing the act. The abuse was so unbearable that detaching themselves from it, as if it were happening to someone else, became a coping method.

Candace, a forty-two-year-old counselor at a battered women's shelter, tells of her reaction to the sexual abuse by her grandfather and later her brother. "I left my body. I don't think I did when my grandfather was first molesting me. I just disconnected from the waist down. With my brother, I remember going down to his room and the dread. And taking off my clothes. And as soon as the clothes were off, I left. That was my coping mechanism. Most of my childhood I was gone. But I don't know where I went. It was a form of death. I figure it's not going to be much of a problem when I actually physically die because I've had so much practice."

Other women have reported using sexualizing as a means of coping. If they could focus on the sexual stimulation, they could somehow not have to bear what was happening to them. Barbara, whom we met earlier, had been sadistically brutalized by her father; she says: "I think I allowed myself to get caught up with the sexual feeling as a way of escaping.... There were times that it was sexually pleasurable or my body responded to him, and I could use those feelings as an escape from what was going on...." Another survivor reinforced that idea. "Romanticizing my relationship with my brother was very helpful." The fact is that children are sexual beings and that it is not uncommon for children to experience sexual sensations during the sexual abuse. Although feeling sexual pleasure is often seen as a betrayal by one's body, it is also a helpful coping mechanism in surviving the sexual assault.

Some women report that animals and dolls were important comforts in their troubled lives. "I had a dog. I had this wonderful collie dog from when I was two until I was thirteen. She followed me everywhere. When it got too bad, I would go outside and bury myself in her and cry and cry and cry." Another survivor says, "I can't think of anything supportive in my childhood, but I had a doll that I still have. I've been carrying it around all my life."

I remember watching an audience of psychotherapists trying to understand how the members of an incest survivors' panel emerged intact from such brutal childhoods. One therapist asked of Barbara, who had been brutalized and raped by her father, "So how is it that you have successfully overcome your traumatic childhood? Is it your determination? Your IQ?" Barbara answered, "I had a wonderful rabbit." Members of the audience shook their heads in disbelief, for surely some other quality had made the difference. However, they did not see that Barbara's ability to love that rabbit, when everything else around her was so hateful and vicious, was her salvation. Animals and dolls provide for many abused children an outlet for expressing and receiving love and warmth where no other outlets exist.

Creative activities are also often helpful. Art, writing, reading, music, and photography have often been instrumental in coping with incest. They provide forms in which the children could express the pain and grief of growing up abused. "I kept a journal. I played a lot of music. I would go into my bedroom and I'd get off into my fantasy world," recalls Pam, a woman who was repeatedly molested by her university professor father. Doris, a twenty-five-year-old disc jockey, explains, "I wrote. I wrote a lot. I wrote fantasies. One story I wrote dealt with incest, trying to make it glamorous. I wrote the opposite of what was going on."

Involvement in the creative arts often continues into adulthood. I have found among my incest survivor clients a large majority of women who use the arts as a way of putting things in perspective. I recall one client who began to understand her healing process through earlier art work, art she created prior to recovering her memory of severe sexual abuse by her five brothers. Her paintings were of women who were fragmented—a leg on one side of the canvas, an arm and head on the other. Additionally she had several paintings of giant eyes. Upon reclaiming childhood memories of the incest, she remembered always trying to hide from her brothers but they were always finding her. She could never escape her brothers' searching eyes.

Running away, and what adults would label "acting-out" behavior, are also used to escape from the childhood horror. Audrey, thirty-six, remembered "acting-out" as a seven-year-old, and being labeled "crazy" by her mother for her childhood behavior. She was afraid that once I heard what she had done, I would agree with her mother's assessment. Audrey explained that her mother had caught her wearing all of her underpants at the same time. Tearfully she said, "See I was a crazy kid. I did things just to get my mother furious." Perhaps without her history of ongoing sexual abuse, her behavior would have seemed strange. However, this was an attempt to use her underpants as protection against the sexual assualt. If her father was able to touch her genitals when she was wearing only one pair of underpants, perhaps eight underpants could protect her from this violation.

Veronica, thirty-one, explains, "I did a lot of acting out when I was younger. There were social workers, psychiatrists. But no one ever asked what was going on with me. Basically they were putting labels on me, telling me what a terrible person I was. My acting out as a kid was related to the sexual abuse. I started a fire in the woods. I was in the fifth grade and I started skipping school. It seems as if social workers and such were always in my life, but I don't know what they were doing other than moving me around and stuff." Although running away and delinquency often cause additional problems for the child-victim, they are ways of expressing her turmoil and attempts at exercising some type of control.

Denial is also an important coping method. It is a defense mechanism that has protected many children from experiences that were too painful to bear. It can take many forms. "I shut down. I didn't think about it on any level," states Joan, a forty-year-old teacher. Like many incest survivors, Joan recognizes this coping method as something that continues to be a part of how she currently negotiates stress.

There are many other ways in which incested children cope with their abuse. All means of coping were developed because they were necessary. Some methods, such as writing, painting, and nurturing animals, were skills that were life supporting and continued to impact positively on the woman-survivor. Others, such as running away, alcohol, and drugs, helped to relieve some of the anguish but were not life-enhancing behaviors. But whether the coping method had a positive result or a negative result, the behaviors themselves were means of salvaging childhoods. They were normal responses to abnormal childhood situations, and no incest survivor can be criticized for the specific ways in which she attempted to make the unbearable bearable. Regardless of how these coping behaviors are perceived, they are essential components in the ability to not give up on life.

The examination of the incest trauma from the perspective of the child would not be complete without looking at family relationships. Incest takes place in the context of families whether or not the perpetrator is a blood relative.

In all my years of working with incest survivors, I have never known incest to occur in a family where there was a strong, positive mother–daughter bond. That is not to blame mothers, for as mentioned previously, sexual violence severs the mother–daughter bond. It is to note that the relationship between mother and daughter plays an important role in the child's risk for abuse.

Let's look at mothers as described by incest survivors. Almost always, mothers in incestuous families are described as weak, frustrated, and isolated. Many times they are physically sick, depressed, or emotionally impaired, and sometimes they are absent through death, divorce, or desertion. Incest survivors generally perceive their mothers to have abandoned them. In many cases, as adults, the incest survivor is more angry at her mother than at the perpetrator. The survivor is angry at her mother for not having protected her. And she is correct—her mother did not protect her. As a feminist, I recognize the powerless mother to be a victim, but as a therapist, I must not let my feminist beliefs interfere with the survivor's necessary process of raging at her unprotective mother. In time, as we examine the family dynamics, the survivor will probably renegotiate her feelings about her mother, but for now, the mother is perceived as uncaring, unprotective, and absent.

Susan, a forty-three-year-old nun, describes her mother: "My mother was a belaborer and a very frightened, lonely person. And she lived for him [father]. She had no friends. She was a very incapable woman who suffocated. I was her accomplishment. When I won a prize or achievement, I brought them home for her."

Barbara's mother was ill most of Barbara's life until her death when Barbara was twelve. "He used to beat the shit out of her. I remember hearing the violence, but I don't recall visually witnessing it. I may have blocked it out. I spent a lot of the time being convinced that her illness protected her from the abuse that I went through and that [because] I was the target she was spared. But in retrospect, I don't think that's true." Since she had a life-threatening illness, clearly, Barbara's mother was incapable of protecting her daughter. But in the eyes of the child, her mother abandoned her to her father's abuse.

Another survivor says about her mother, "I was her caretaker. She was depressed, suicidal. She was fatalistic. She was dependent on family for social support."

In some incestuous families, mothers are physically or emotionally abusive. I know of one woman who, after years of working on her history of sexual abuse, is just beginning to look at her relationship with her mother. At one of our earlier sessions, she explained that when she was about eighteen months old, her hip was dislocated because she squirmed while her mother was giving her a spanking. When I pursued with her the notion that children do not dislocate their hips by squirming, she began to recall the years of physical abuse at the hands of her mother. In many respects, this survivor's recovery process has been compounded by the physical and emotional abuse she suffered at the hands of her mother. Because of the powerful control her mother had over her, she has had difficulty feeling anger toward her. Yet it also became clear, as we examined the dynamics of this family, that this abusive mother was acting out her own feelings of powerlessness and that she was and continues to be isolated and depressed. The mother's powerlessness is not an excuse for her abusiveness. Abuse is abuse. However, it appears that in those cases where mothers are physically or emotionally abusive, they are usually powerless people in the family system. And although there are cases of violent, abusive mothers, most incestuous families contain a weak, ineffectual, or absent mother.

Fathers look much different. When the father is the perpetrator, he is usually domineering, controlling, and in conflict with other family members. Even when fathers are not the perpetrators, they are often tyrannical and/or emotionally distant. Annette, abused by her grandfather, describes her relationship with her father. "My friend [a childhood friend] said that she thought the horrible fights my father and I had were because he was the one who wanted to molest me. She said that I was very sexual as a child. It's true. I was fully grown at thirteen. And my parents had a clearly frustrated sexual life. He was just enraged totally all the time about my sexuality." Although not the overt perpetrator, Annette's father was a destructive force within the family. He attempted to control the family through anger, rage, and a variety of unpredictable emotional outbursts. Additionally he may have been a seductive father who did not overtly act on his sexual feelings for his daughter. Yet she was aware of his fury toward her budding sexuality.

Besides being controlling, abusive, and emotionally distant, fathers in incestuous families are often divisive within families. They play one family member against the other and often thrive within the family because they divide and conquer. With mothers being emotionally separated from their daughters, and siblings being disconnected or at odds, the perpetrator father more easily gains access to his child. In many cases, fathers begin the sexual abuse with the oldest daughter and work their way through the rest of the children. Keeping siblings emotionally apart allows for the father to move through his family without any constraints or consequences. Even when fathers are not perpetrators, incestuous families are often disconnected and fragmented. Yet an incestuous family, more often than not, appears to the outside world to be a good, nuclear family. And that is not surprising, because an incestuous family is usually a closed system—that is, a family that is insular and does not allow outsiders to enter their network. Without entry, those outside the system cannot assess the real dynamics of the family. Additionally, these closed systems often appear to be quite safe and loving. Family members may be churchgoers and the father a respected man in the community.

Children in incestuous families are powerless. They are often isolated from each other and from the outside world. If siblings do have a comradeship, it is usually the result of attempting to survive an embattled relationship with the father. Although all children are viewed as token people within the family, girls in particular are not valued as human beings. Rebecca, sexually abused by her father, brother, and uncles, tells of the role she played in her family. "I was the baby. I was very unimportant in this family. I was the baby, and I was the girl, so I was considered extra baggage. My father used to say to me that I was an afterthought, implying that I was an accident. I was a miserably unhappy kid, and I guess that I loved them all very much because kids do. Yet I was pretty timid with all of these people because they could have rejected me like that [snaps her fingers]. My whole existence was on a string. My whole reason for apparently being there was to be pretty. I had to look impeccable all the time."

The incestuous family profile is fairly consistent. Regardless of race, class, ethnicity, or political persuasion, incestuous families look the same. The pattern that emerges is of a closed system in which what appears to the outside world to be a wonderful family is in fact a family with an ill, alcoholic, battered, emotionally or physically absent mother who is ruled by fear and manipulated by a divisive, domineering father. I propose, moreover, that the family dynamics of the incestuous family are dynamics that closely resemble those of the "ideal" nuclear family. Almost everything within mainstream culture—the media, churches, schools, the courts—supports this model in which the father is the head of the household, the mother passively implements the father's commands, and the children are powerless. It is clear that when families are modeled after this patriarchal paradigm, children are at risk. Our models of families must change in order to protect children from sexual violence.

There is no doubt that living within an incestuous family leaves scars on all its victims/survivors. In my years of working with incest survivors, I have learned one especially important thing: there is no such thing as "better" or "worse" incest. Incest is incest—devastating no matter what degree of brutality is involved. A child seduced by an attentive, reward-giving adult may feel sexual pleasure and emotional pleasure and may enjoy the secondary gains of gifts, attention, money, or praise, but seductive rape can lead to terrible confusion in later life as to whether she was complicitous in the incestuous act—unlike violent rapes, which leave their scars but leave no doubt about the act being unwanted and unsolicited. There is a tendency to focus on the most brutal cases of incestuous rape when presenting a picture of the destructiveness of incest, but this is a disservice to the many more women who were sexually abused in ways that led them to doubt the legitimacy of their pain. Most cases of incest are not torturous. Yet I know of no incest survivor, regardless of the degree of violence, who has been left unscarred.

My work with survivors has shown me that scars are necessary for the healing process to begin. Scars must not be considered synonymous with hopelessness and an inability to recover but rather as signs that one has made it through a terrible ordeal. Incest is traumatic, and it leaves scars. We must celebrate those scars.

CHAPTER FIVE

Healing

Women can and do heal from incest. The recovery process takes place over time, and includes necessary stages that must be mastered; however, there is no one "correct" process that must be followed. Some therapists, primarily feminist therapists, state that incest survivors must heal the mother–daughter bond in order to recover; others say that incest survivors must confront their perpetrators in order to recover; still others state that incest survivors must participate in incest recovery groups in order to heal. Each of these steps is often very helpful in the recovery process, but I believe that we do a great disservice to incest survivors when we prescribe a set formula they must follow. In my research with incest survivors, I have known women who have confronted their perpetrators and others who have not. I have known women who have carefully and deliberately worked on their relationships with their mothers and others who chose to distance from them. There are women who have moved clear across the country to get away from their families and others who live in the same town. Though there are specific stages survivors must master, there are no specific steps that must be taken to get through each stage. There is no formula for healing. Women have facilitated their recovery process in many different ways.

It is also important to understand that incest recovery is a spiral process rather than a linear one. There are times when one makes it through a stage only to return to it later, but the second time around the stage is experienced in a different way, generally with more insight and clarity. When an earlier stage is reexperienced the survivor is often troubled because she feels that she is going backward. During these times I remind my clients of the progress they have made and the strengths they are now bringing to this period in their lives. I also remind them that healing does not necessarily happen in a straight-line continuum and that what they are doing and experiencing is their process and needs to be honored.

In some ways, incest recovery follows the stages of dying as described by Elisabeth Kübler-Ross, the famed psychiatrist and author of *On Death and Dying* (1969). Kübler-Ross suggests that people facing life-threatening illnesses go through a series of steps, beginning with denial and isolation and moving on through anger, bargaining, depression, and acceptance. I believe that these steps are also part of the incest recovery process; however, they are only *part* of incest recovery. They don't necessarily take place in that order, and in the recovery process other stages follow. And although the process itself might feel like a death to the survivor engaged in it, mastering these stages ends not in death but rather in more fully experiencing life. The stages of incest recovery are acknowledgment, the crisis, disclosure (to oneself and to others), depression, anger, mourning, acceptance, and moving on.

ACKNOWLEDGMENT

Unlike in the process of dying, in incest recovery, I believe, denial precedes the first step. Incest survivors use denial in many forms: they may have no memory of the sexual abuse, they may minimize the effects of the abuse, they may minimize the actual abuse itself and/or not believe their perception of what took place—for example, they may believe that they are making up the story of incest. Denial is a defense mechanism that helps protect the survivor from the psychic pain that will accompany the acknowledgment that she was, in fact, sexually abused as a child. Denial initially is a necessary defense mechanism, but it must be given up in order to allow healing to begin. Thus, acknowledging that the incest happened, although she may not label it "incest," is the first step toward recovery. She knows that *something* happened.

Often, remembering that incest occurred results from trigger points. Trigger points are events, circumstances, catalysts that set off either specific memories or general feelings that something traumatic happened during childhood. Trigger points may include the birth of the survivor's baby, the survivor's child reaching the age at which the survivor was first sexually abused, the death of the perpetrator, an anniversary date, a color, a smell, a season. A trigger point can be anything that triggers a realization that something occurred during childhood. Debra, age thirty-five, had her first memory of her father's ongoing sexual assaults as she was driving home from his funeral. Until his death, she had no memory of the abuse. His death set off a flood of memories, nightmares, and flashbacks. As we worked together, Debra began to understand that until her father's death, she did not feel safe enough to remember. Only after her father's death was she able to reclaim her childhood memories. Our psyches have great ways of protecting us from what we cannot emotionally handle. Although the memories, nightmares, and flashbacks were difficult for Debra to cope with, they were signs that she was ready to deal with the incest and to actively begin the recovery process.

For Debra, the trigger point was the death of her perpetrator. For others, it may be an anniversary date or season. If the abuse began around Halloween, for instance, autumn or colorful leaves or seeing children dressed in Halloween costumes may trigger a memory. Or if the perpetrator smelled of tobacco or always wore blue, that familiar smell or color may be the catalyst for memory.

THE CRISIS

Once the incest is acknowledged and recognized as sexual abuse, a crisis, often accompanied by some form of isolation, takes place. This is what Ellen Bass and Laura Davis (1988) aptly call "the emergency state." This stage often hits as a major crisis. The survivor thinks about the incestuous abuse continuously. Often the survivor appears to be obsessive in her focus on incest and its effects on her. She may read everything that she can get her hands on about incest and sexual violence. She may constantly talk about the abuse. She may withdraw from those people in her life whom she feels cannot or will not join her in her quest to find out what really happened to her as a child. This may cause temporary and sometimes permanent damage to the relationships in her life because she may feel abandoned by those people who do not relate to her determination to know all that there is to know about incest. She may feel that her friends and partners cannot understand what she is going through. She may need to be left alone by her family and friends. Her partners and friends may not understand her process and may feel abandoned by the survivor.

In addition to the planned focus on the incest, unwanted elements of this process may also occur, such as flashbacks, nightmares, anxiety attacks, depression, suicidal ideation, withdrawal, and loss of interest in other aspects of one's life. This is often a very scary time for the incest survivor. It is a time when support is essential and when social networking is the most difficult yet the most necessary. Incest survivor support groups and incest recovery therapy are very important. The crisis stage may last several days or it may last several years. Regardless of its length or intensity, this is a time for survivors to reach out for help and for their friends and families to be supportive, nurturing, and understanding. During this time I remind clients that they have already lived through the worst—the actual incest itself—and that things will get better. However, on many levels this present crisis feels as bad, if not worse, than the actual childhood experience, because as a child the survivor's coping methods protected her from feeling the pain. Therefore during this period we need to rev up as many life-enhancing coping skills as possible. These may include ongoing therapy, survivor networks, painting and drawing, writing, self-pampering (massage, facials, saunas, etc.), jogging, walking, other forms of exercise, gardening, meditation, deep breathing, and other positive ways that the survivor can get support and comfort. This is a time when the survivor needs to be good to herself and to really take care of herself. It is important for her to remember that this state, as bad as it feels, is only temporary and that things will get better. This is a time to remind survivors of their strengths, their coping mechanisms, and their social networks; it is also a time when I, as a therapist, am especially available for emergency phone calls and appointments. It is important for survivors during this stage to use every means possible to continue.

DISCLOSURE: TELLING MYSELF/TELLING ANOTHER

During the crisis state, which occurs when the survivor first acknowledges that sexual abuse has occurred, she begins to *believe* that what she is remembering was in fact sexual abuse. This is what I call "telling myself." The survivor discloses to herself that she is in fact an incest survivor. Once she has disclosed to herself, she may go back and forth between believing and denying: one day she believes the sexual abuse really happened, and the next day she thinks she is making it up. In time she will mostly believe herself, and someday she will completely believe that sexual abuse occurred. Self-disclosure is an important step. It is generally followed by telling someone else.

Thus the survivor proceeds from "telling myself" to "telling another." This disclosure—breaking the silence—is an important and empowering, yet scary, step.

Breaking the silence, telling the secret that she has been carrying with her for years and years, is crucial. Most survivors have kept the secret out of fear. It is the type of fear children feel when perpetrators warn them of the dreadful consequences that will occur if they ever tell. These consequences may include the perpetrator going to jail, the child going to foster care, the mother being angry, the mother being killed, the child being killed. I remember one adolescent with whom I worked who was told by her father (the perpetrator)that he would burn down the house with her family members inside if she ever told anyone. It is with the intensity of those childhood fears that the adult survivor now breaks her silence. The fear is as profound for her now as it was, back then, for the child victim she was. The release can be empowering; the anticipation can be dreadful.

I believe that it is essential for therapists to ask every client during intake in a nonpejorative, nonjudgmental way if the client as a child ever had sex with an adult. Some women who were sexually abused as children may not identify sex with an adult as abuse, therefore they are able to answer yes to a nonpejorative question about sex with an adult but not to a question about incest or other forms of childhood sexual abuse. Some survivors initially will not be able to answer the question because of intense fear but later in therapy may have the resources to examine it. Therefore, the question needs to be raised. If the therapist does not ask early in the therapy relationship, she or he may never find out. By asking, the therapist may help the survivor, who may be frozen by fear, to disclose. Telling another is an important step in this healing journey.

After disclosing to another individual or to a group, the survivor often feels many emotions—fear, shame, guilt, sadness, anger, joy, power, doubt. She will feel different emotions at different times. It is not uncommon for the survivor, after having made her disclosure, to go back to doubting her perception and her memory and return to a state in which she does not believe that the sexual abuse happened. She may tell you that she made the story up and that nothing really happened to her as a child. When this occurs with my clients, I ask, "So why would you make this up? Why not make up a story about how wonderful your childhood was?" The truth is that the childhood sexual abuse was not made up. What is happening is a direct result of the disclosure, for the survivor feels disloyal to the perpetrator and the family within which the sexual abuse occurred. With support and encouragement, the survivor can work through the emotions that keep her in the denial stage—sadness, guilt, disloyalty, shame, and so on.

DEPRESSION

During these early stages of incest recovery, the survivor may feel a profound depression. She may feel suicidal. In addition to needing a supportive network, on some occasions she may need psychiatric intervention via medication (antidepressants) or hospitalization. In my work with incest survivors, medication is indicated in some cases, and hospitalization has been an option on a few occasions. Although many survivors can work through this state of depression without medication or hospitalization, I believe it is important to acknowledge these options and to see them as ways of overcoming profound grief and sadness. Additionally, on those occasions when psychiatric intervention is warranted, it should not be perceived as a failure but rather as a life-affirming decision. Survivors must do whatever life-enhancing tasks are necessary to work through the recovery process. The goal is to go from survivor to thriver.

The depression state is also a temporary state. Things will be better as the survivor continues through the stages. But while the depression exists, the survivor needs to take care of herself. She needs to reach out to supportive people. This is the time when it is especially important for her to have an incest survivor network: an incest recovery therapy group, a self-help group, supportive friends, partners, professionals, and so on. This is not the time for her "to go it alone." Support persons need to be encouraging, empathetic, good listeners, nurturing, and available, and survivors need to be reminded that they are strong, motivated women. They need to be reminded that they must not give up hope, because things will get better.

ANGER

Depression is followed by anger. Although in fact anger is present in the preceding stages as well, it is usually unacknowledged, turned inward, or in other ways avoided. For some survivors, anger is ever present but misdirected and focused on, for example, children, spouses, lovers, partners, friends. Anger is a toxic area for all women in our culture, and it is particularly toxic for incest survivors. In women in general, anger is commonly trivialized at best or punished at worst. It is seen as emotional, irrational, unwarranted, and petty and is often met with scorn, insult, or violence. For incest survivors, anger is even more difficult and dangerous because, more often than not, anger within the incestuous family of origin was violent, explosive, and damaging; role models of anger were scary and destructive. Thus incest survivors often do not know how to deal with the anger they feel. As children, they were not able to express their outrage at what was happening to them; as adults, they are often afraid of their anger. They associate anger with violence and destruction and believe that if they get angry they will be out of control. They fear that if they express it, their anger will escalate to rage and be unstoppable. The job for incest survivors, then, is to learn to identify their anger and to express it in empowering ways. Anger expressed as violence is not empowering but rather demeaning and shameful, and incest survivors must learn appropriate ways of expressing anger. They need to understand that we are not in control of our emotions but we are in control of our behaviors, that it is not anger that must be controlled but rather how we express it that must be managed.

Before one learns to express anger in a life-enhancing way, one must be able to identify it. I sometimes ask my clients to draw a continuum of anger, with annoyance at the beginning and rage at the end. They must fill in the middle with the degrees of anger they can identify. The continuum might look like this:

+annoyance ——— disturbance ——— irritation ——— anger ——— fury ——— rage+

This is the first step to learning the forms anger can take in one's life. From here, I might ask the client to identify the different degrees of anger she felt in the course of a day. What happened? What was felt? How did she know what she was feeling? Where on the continuum of anger did it fall? How soon did she know what she was feeling? What body cues did she experience that helped her to identify the feeling? How did she express the feeling? For some clients, learning to know what anger feels like is an important step. After she can identify anger, we then generate ways of expressing it. Specific activities and exercises to identify and express anger are important in helping the survivor to utilize this important emotion. This will be discussed more fully in chapter 9. The point here is that anger, present throughout the process even if unacknowledged, unnoticed, or misdirected, is an important stage unto itself. Being able to express it is healing, often a catharsis, and additional healing stages can proceed.

Often when the survivor is in the midst of the anger stage, the issue of confrontation comes up. Should the survivor confront her perpetrator or not? Should the survivor confront or disclose to her family or not? There is no general right answer to these questions. But there are individual right answers. Confrontations and disclosures are personal decisions that need to be made by each individual survivor.

Sometimes the survivor feels that a confrontation would cause her too much pain and turmoil, that she needs to protect her elderly parents from her terrible secret, that her confrontation would do irreparable damage to the family, that her rage will become uncontrollable, or that her perpetrator is still too powerful in her life and in the life of her family. Sometimes the perpetrator is dead, and confrontation seems impossible. These issues are all valid, and the survivor is the expert on what she needs to do. However, I believe that confrontation is always a later option. Healing can take place without confrontation, but the absence of confrontation leaves the survivor with an incomplete issue—an important piece of her life that remains unmentioned. Having an incomplete issue does not mean healing can't take place. It may or may not be felt as a barrier between her and her family members.

Often during the anger stage the survivor may decide that she needs to confront her perpetrator or her family in order to get relief from the rage that she is feeling. She feels that she is carrying around a family secret and its weight is no longer bearable. A confrontation can alleviate the burden of years and years of shame, guilt, anger, and secrecy. The importance of a confrontation is in the relief it gives to the confronter. It is important that the confrontation be planned and thought out, because its success depends on the survivor's rather than the perpetrator's response. When planning a confrontation the survivor needs to be prepared for anything. Though it is often the wish of the survivor to have the perpetrator admit the sexual abuse and apologize for his behavior, more times than not the perpetrator denies the abuse and family members side with him. I know of one woman, Margaret, who told her seventy-year-old mother that she had been sexually abused for years by Margaret's father. Her mother said nothing at the time, but weeks later she wrote to her daughter, "You have ruined my golden years by what you have said. How can I forgive you?" Although Margaret never sees her mother and has rarely spoken to her since then, she feels that the confrontation was extremely empowering and was a necessary part of her healing.

What makes the confrontation successful is that the survivor changes the dynamics in the family. The survivor is no longer responding to someone else's rules but is rather setting the limits and determining how to be in her family. Although it may be nice to have perpetrators admit to their wrongs and apologize for their behavior, or for families to be supportive of the survivor, that is not a prerequisite for a successful confrontation. The air is cleared, the secret is exploded, the weight of the burden removed, and the relational dynamics have shifted—the confrontation has been successful.

If this step is to be taken, support networks should be in place. The confrontation can be done via letter, by phone, or in person. It can take place in the survivor's therapist's office, at the home of a friend, in a public place. It is usually best to have the confrontation in a neutral place but most importantly in a place where the survivor feels safe. It is also important for the survivor to have a safe, nurturing place to be immediately after the confrontation. The confrontation can act as a catharsis and can leave the survivor tired and drained, or it can result in a burst of energy followed by an emotional letdown; either way, it's essential that the survivor plan not only the confrontation itself but also what she will do after the confrontation.

In working with clients on the issue of confrontations, then, I underscore several points. The first and foremost is that a confrontation's success is determined by the survivor's response, not the perpetrator's. Second, preparation is essential. I always ask my clients a great number of questions, among them: What do you want to say? How will you say it? Where will the confrontation take place? What are your fantasies about how your perpetrator/family will respond? What is the worst thing that could happen? What vehicle will you use for this confrontation (letter, phone, in person, etc.)? Where will you go, and whom will you be with, after the confrontation? My one caution is to not plan for a confrontation during already emotionally charged events, such as Christmas, New Year's, Thanksgiving.

Shirley, age forty-four, confronted her mother about Shirley's childhood abuse by a baby sitter. Her mother had a distant and detached relationship with all her children underscored by the fact that Shirley and her siblings lived on the west coast and their mother in Quebec. Her siblings warned Shirley that her mother would not be able to hear Shirley's anger at her mother for not being aware that something was happening and for not protecting her. Perhaps because of these warnings, Shirley was able to understand that the confrontation would be successful because she would change because of the confrontation, not because her mother would change. When she was preparing for the confrontation, including deciding how and when she would confront, I asked Shirley what the worst consequences of a confrontation might be. She came up with numerous possibilities—her mother being angry or defensive or minimizing the effects of the abuse, dismissing Shirley's feelings, severing the already limited relationship that they had. I asked her how it would be if her mother tried to become closer and more open with her because of the confrontation. Any change in a relationship, even a positive one, can be unsettling and I wanted to help prepare her for that possibility as well. That was something Shirley had not thought of, and when examining that prospect, she began to prepare for what might be her mother's attempt at getting closer and possibly "smothering" Shirley. As it turned out, the confrontation—done initially by letter, followed up by a phone call, and later continued in person—was seen as successful by Shirley because in addition to her mother apologizing for her lack of protection, Shirley was prepared for her mother's attempt to solidify their weak, distant relationship. Shirley was strong enough to secure her boundaries and to set limits on her relationship with her mother.

Grace, on the other hand, prepared for a family confrontation about the sexual abuse by her stepfather. She planned the confrontation—when and where and how it was to be done. She said that the worst that could happen would be that her family would align themselves with the stepfather, but she said that she could deal with that. Grace forged ahead with the confrontation without clearly understanding what it would mean to her if her family did not reject her stepfather. Although her family members believed her, the fact that her mother remains married to the stepfather and her siblings still associate with him causes Grace to feel betrayed and abandoned. Somehow, in spite of talking about the possible results of confrontation, she had not been fully prepared for her family's response to her disclosure; she had needed more preparation and help with the confrontation process, to not only intellectually understand but be emotionally prepared for what she deemed the worst possible scenario for the family confrontation.

MOURNING

After the anger stage, whether or not it is followed by a confrontation, there is often a period of mourning during which the survivor experiences extreme sadness. This seems to differ from the depression stage. The sadness is often an emotional letdown after empowering yet difficult work. Because individuals experience catharsis at different times, the women in my incest recovery groups take turns feeling empowered and uplifted and then overwhelmingly sad. This happens for several reasons, probably the most understandable of which is that once the anger and rage are worked through, the survivor is able to get in touch with her deeper feelings. The sadness was covered by the anger, just as the anger was covered by the earlier depression. With the anger diminished, the survivor can now grieve for her lost childhood and feel sad for that little girl who was not allowed to thrive. At times, this can manifest itself as a profound sadness. The survivor might feel as if she were going backward, believing that she felt this sadness before and had hoped that this grief was behind her. In fact, this is truly a different stage, a necessary stage, one that will lead the way to better understanding of herself as a child and as the adult she has become. She has become free to feel deep pain and to mourn for the little girl who was betrayed.

This sadness is the result of hard work. It is similar to what one feels after having completed a monumental project, the letdown feeling that often follows the initial feelings of relief and pride—these initial feelings are very intense but cannot be sustained indefinitely; a moment of disillusionment inevitably follows. Thus the sadness is a natural development as one passes through a process that includes extreme emotions, difficult stages, and a tremendous amount of psychic energy. It's an announcement of another stage completed.

Another way to understand the sadness positively is to see that sadness is a normal, necessary emotion that all human beings experience. Sadness is not an emotion to avoid at all costs but, rather, an indication that someone is engaging in life, life that by its nature must be filled with accomplishments and disappointments. Thus the ability to feel sadness is the ability to take a chance on life; and feeling even the profound sadness of this stage should not be perceived as sliding backward in the recovery process. During this time I remind my clients that life is full of ups and downs and that a complete life is not sorrow-free. The fact that they can now be in touch with their sadness is a wonderful step, for they now can begin to feel the entire spectrum of emotions—from profound sadness to ecstatic joy. These words are not meant to short-circuit the sadness/grief stage but rather to give encouragement to the survivor as she goes through another difficult period of incest recovery.

ACCEPTANCE

The sadness/mourning stage is followed by acceptance, a stage of letting go, or making peace with the past. This is not an acceptance of incest as a phenomenon but rather of the fact that the incest happened, of the effects it had and continues to have, of the fact that the survivor was not to blame, and that there is no changing what occurred. As Amy, thirty-three years old, says, "It's raw stuff, and I have to bring it out and put it in its place. It's never gonna change. It will always be my history. But I want it to be my history and not my present."

Before letting go of the past, the survivor generally renegotiates her place within the family. She is now different within this family. She may distance herself and move clear across the country to get away from it. She may continue to live in the same town but now as a visible, effective member of it. She may have confronted the perpetrator or family. She may not have. But in all cases, she accepts her family to be what they are without being swallowed up by them. She knows that the perpetrator no longer has power over her. She is an autonomous adult, no longer a dependent child.

This is not to say that the survivor who has made peace with her past will not at times reexperience old emotions and reactions because of the sexual abuse. At times, memories, fears, anger, sadness will be restimulated, and this may momentarily feel like a major setback. However, she will handle the restimulation of this trauma. She will go on. She has made peace with the past.

Acceptance, or making peace with the past, does not imply forgiving the perpetrator. Forgiveness is not a prerequisite for recovery from childhood sexual abuse; there are different ways to make peace. For some survivors, forgiving their perpetrators has helped them to let go, while others have not forgiven, and cannot forgive, their perpetrators. There is no right or wrong in this matter. One need not forgive one's abuser or one's family in order to heal. Some atrocities may very well be unforgivable.

If any forgiveness is necessary for the recovery process to continue it is forgiving oneself that is essential. The survivor needs to forgive herself for not making it stop, for not telling anyone, for not being believed, for being small, for responding sexually, for acquiring life-threatening skills, for being victimized, for modeling the abusive behavior with smaller children, for being revictimized, for not protecting her children, for marrying an abuser, for drinking, drugging, overeating, for not being perfect. This forgiveness is necessary, to reach the acceptance stage.

Acceptance is a process in which the survivor puts the incest into perspective; she "puts it in its place." She understands and acknowledges that the incest occurred, that it was not her fault, that there was nothing she could have done to prevent it, and that whether her body responded sexually or not, she did not want or choose the incestuous relationship. When she has reached the acceptance stage, the survivor has let go of the notion that her family will be different or that it will ever be the family that she wanted and needed, and she no longer expects any compensation from the perpetrator or her family for her lost childhood. She may experience the range of emotions that she has buried regarding the incest—depression, guilt, anger, rage, sadness—but she accepts them as emotions that occur in the course of life.

Survivors have reported many ways they have let go of the sexual abuse. Taking care of the hurt child within; attending to the hurt adult; spirituality, particularly nonpatriarchal spirituality; taking on a survivor's mission—making the recovery a gift and the impetus for devoting oneself to the creation of a world that is a safer and better place; becoming involved with women's groups that are not focused on sexual abuse; becoming involved in the creative arts; creating "letting go" rituals; all of these and more have been mentioned by survivors as means of letting go of the past and moving on to the future. Acceptance, with its letting go of the past, does not imply that there are no scars from this childhood trauma. As mentioned previously, scars remain after one heals from any major injury. Incest will always be part of a survivor's history. But as Amy says, ". . . let the past have its own death and be gone. I am very much here in the present."

MOVING ON

There is something beyond the acceptance stage. It has been called the "integration stage," the "moving-on stage," the "going-beyond stage." This is the stage, perhaps the final stage of healing, in which the survivor recognizes that being an incest survivor is only one piece of her. She realizes that, yes, she is a survivor, but she is also a woman, a lover, a friend, a mother, a professional, an advocate, a whole person. Often this stage is the result of taking on the "survivor's mission," and making her recovery from the abuse she suffered as a child, a gift—using her power as a survivor to make a difference in the world. This may mean working with sexually abused children, working in a battered women's shelter, working for a crime victim's program, working in sexual abuse prevention programs, but in all cases, the commitment to making the world a better, safer place for women and children has helped many survivors become thrivers.

Taking on the survivor's mission is an important step in the recovery process, but it is a step that can be taken only when the survivor is ready. Becoming involved in emotionally charged areas, such as the prevention or healing of wife battering, rape, incest, or child battering, can be toxic for a survivor who has not put her own abuse in perspective. Even when a survivor is ready to work on her survivor's mission, she should continue to get support and supervision for the issues that may arise within her. A support network can be very helpful as the survivor continues to change herself and the world.

In addition to work that is part of the survivor's mission, I encourage survivors to become involved with organizations that are not related to sexual abuse. For instance, women who have been involved in incest recovery groups can benefit from joining a feminist reading group or a political women's group or finding other ways of networking with women in diverse group settings. This is an important step in moving beyond being an incest survivor, which is an important part of her life story but is not all of her. I want my clients to honor their histories as incest survivors but also to cultivate the other strong, wonderful parts of them, parts that make them the complete individuals they are. When a woman can do this, she has mastered the difficult journey from victim to survivor to thriver.

CHAPTER SIX

Collective Denial

In my work with incest survivors, I have learned not only what helps promote healing but also what impedes the incest recovery process. What seems to be most detrimental is what I call "collective denial." This occurs when helping professionals, family members, and/or friends minimize the incest, deny that incest has occurred, do not respect the incest survivor's healing process, or accept the notion that sex between an adult and a child is not harmful.

Collective denial in which physicians, teachers, nurses, psychotherapists, and other helping professionals do not listen to stories of sexual abuse or do not investigate the reasons for children's behaviors has long existed and continues to exist today. Annette, age forty, says, "Every time in therapy I bring it [incest] up, no one wants to attend to it. The child psychiatrist I saw as a child, a very reputable one—I cried, I remember, in her office and told her how bad I felt and a lot of stuff about being confused and guilty. And she turned around and said, 'That was fine.' I've never understood."

Sometimes the discomfort of the listener causes her or him to dismiss the incest issue. A listener who is a woman may not be able to bear hearing the stories of incest because she may not be able to bear her own feelings of terror at knowing that as a woman, she, too, is vulnerable to sexual violence. And since one out of three women have been sexually abused by an adult before the age of eighteen, a woman therapist may have her own incest recovery issues stirred up. If she has not worked through her own recovery process, she may have difficulty attending to the incest, acknowledging its importance in the lives of women, or accepting the fact that specific healing steps must be taken.

On the other hand, a listener who is a man may not be able to hear his clients talk about incest; he may instead deny the traumatic effects it has had, because he may identify with the perpetrator, and he may also be aroused by the details of the incestuous act. A male therapist may also have trouble hearing expressions of anger toward men and thus be unable to facilitate this necessary process. Of course, there is also always the danger that a male therapist has internalized the patriarchal view of women and children as sexual objects who exist for men's pleasure.

Denial, no matter what the explanation, is, of course, extremely detrimental to the girl-victim or woman-survivor. Clearly it is criminal for adults to dismiss stories of sexual abuse of children or neglect to follow through on the cues that signal that abuse has taken place. Yet incest survivors have told me many stories of how their childhood attempts at getting help went unheeded.

Candace tells of her school experience: "The P.E. teacher would hold my skirt with a baton as if I was some disgusting creature. And if I was bruised, she'd say, 'You don't have to get dressed for gym today.' But she'd never ask."

Erica, age twenty-nine, says, "My teachers ignored my signals. I hung around after school and wanted special attention. I was too terrified of acting out or failing. Instead I looked pathetic and hung around people. Somehow they should have thought, This kid needs help, or What's behind this? But no one asked."

Margaret, age forty, adds, "I was out of school for six months, they didn't ask, Why is she getting sick so often?"

Teachers are not the only ones who are in a position to intercede for children and often do not. Family physicians have done their share of denying. Although doctors generally do not get adequate training about child sexual abuse, many times the signs of sexual abuse are obvious; yet they aren't addressed. Family physicians may suspect sexual abuse but hesitate to intervene because they feel protective of their relationship with the family or because they are concerned that their involvement may have them tied up for days in court. Sometimes doctors, like many people, believe that incest is a family matter in which they shouldn't get involved.

Barbara tells of one trip to the doctor, when he saw bruises on her body: "My doctor sent my parents out of the room and asked where I got the bruises, and I told him my father beat me. The pediatrician stayed in the room staring at me with a very angry look on his face until I recanted the story, and then he went out to get my parents and bring them back into the room." She was sent home with her parents without any intervention by the physician. Barbara, a scientist, has since obtained her childhood medical records. Her medical history clearly details numerous injuries and illnesses that could only indicate childhood sexual abuse. She is actively working to eliminate such medical negligence so this will not happen to another child.

Amy, age thirty-three, recalls, "My family doctor was always checking my genitals. He never said anything—just always checked my genitals." Amy believes that the doctor saw the signs of abuse but did nothing.

Pam, age thirty-five, tells of her adult encounter with a school nurse who was not available to her when she needed her. "I tried to tell the school nurse one time. I thought about telling her—it seemed like people were fake. They all had these little value systems and all but don't come near *me* with it. She remembers that I wanted to tell, also. [Later] I saw her at an incest training at the hospital, and she came up to me and said, 'You know, I remember once you coming to me, and it looked like you wanted to say something to me.' She was really surprised to see me there [at the incest training] and said, 'Now I know what it was.'"

Missing cues, outright denying the truth of incest stories, acknowledging that abuse did in fact occur but acting as if it does not need to be addressed—these are all ways that helping professionals have turned their backs on young victims and adult survivors. Helping professionals can make a difference in stopping the sexual abuse from continuing for children and in facilitating the recovery process for women. But many times they do not.

In most cases, children who are being sexually abused give signs that they are being abused. Children often tell in behaviors what they can't say in words. If adults who work with children look more closely at these cues and intervene, many children may be rescued from family violence and abuse. Signs of childhood sexual abuse include a sudden radical change in behavior, sudden change in school grades, self-destructive behavior, destructive behavior to others, extremes in behavior including being aggressive or withdrawn, poor social relations, seductive behavior, sexual knowledge beyond their age, public masturbation, sexual abuse of smaller children or animals, regressive behavior, runaway or delinquent behavior, depression, suicidal ideation or gestures, refusing to change for gym, and wearing clothes that cover the body when not appropriate for the season, climate, or activity. When these signs are ignored, helping professionals and other adults engage in collective denial.

Some adults in authority are particularly damaging to children, especially incested children, because they have themselves bought into patriarchal values and actively impose these values on children. Barbara tells of an encounter she had in school: "We exchanged little Valentine's messages on St. Valentine's Day when I was in the seventh grade. I got a note that looked like the teacher's handwriting, although I'll never know, because it was anonymous, but it said, 'Define femininity, now practice it.' Now maybe this was supposed to be some helpful, anonymous advice, and I'd like to think that it wasn't [meant to be] destructive. But it was grossly damaging, because here I am and I'm not even trying to be feminine, and I was getting my ass ripped off and this person wants me to be feminine, and this conflict was just another failure." Barbara was probably correct that the card was from a teacher—what seventh-grader writes notes like that? What we are seeing is an adult teacher who had internalized the patriarchal model of what a girl or woman should be and was imposing that on a student. What might have been intended as helpful advice to a budding adolescent was in fact another blow to her development. Whatever the teacher's definition of femininity was, Barbara was not meeting it. Thus a child who had no support system within her family had lost another avenue for positive involvement with an adult because of his or her arbitrary values of maleness and femaleness. Was this more detrimental to Barbara because she was an incest survivor? Perhaps. What gave rise to this "helpful bit of advice" was that Barbara was perhaps not flirtatious, seductive, or helpless enough to be considered feminine. This was a troublesome bit of news for a girl who was being battered and raped regularly by her father. What more could happen if she were flirtatious, seductive, or helpless?

The collective denial that victims of incest experience as children often continues for adult survivors, and it can be just as destructive. What can be particularly painful during the recovery process is the denial engaged in by the survivor's family members, friends, partners, spouses, and therapists. Another quote from Barbara illustrates this point. "My stepsister said that he [father] was only trying to show he loved me, and my stepmother says they are my fantasies of what I wanted. He slept with me after my mother died to comfort me." It is devastating for a survivor to finally disclose to another human being that she was sexually abused as a child and be met with disbelief. She may feel invalidated and begin to doubt her memories of what took place as a child. She may feel depressed, angry, and invisible. If this happens, hopefully the adult survivor will find a network that will support her in her recovery process. If she feels that she cannot detach completely from those who do not support her in her healing process, she needs to at least eliminate them from that aspect of her life. During the recovery process she should not have to convince other people or attempt to convince them of what happened. What is important is that she herself believes that the incest took place and that she fill her life with people who will enhance her recovery process rather than impede it.

The survivor's need to avoid contact with people who are engaged in denial of her incestuous past does not apply only to family members and friends. Sometimes family physicians and even psychotherapists minimize the sexual abuse and its effects on the survivor. The medical and mental health professions have a long history of denying incest and other forms of childhood sexual abuse. We need only to recall Freud and his followers. It is not surprising that this denial continues even today. Therefore the survivor may have to pick and choose before she finds a psychotherapist who believes that incest took place, that incest is traumatic, and that incest recovery is possible. She must also be careful and critical when she chooses other helping professionals, physicians, massage therapists, chiropractors, and other body workers, who also need to be sensitive to the issues the survivor brings to her appointments. If a helping professional minimizes the effects of the sexual assault or does not respond sensitively and appropriately to the survivor's issues about touch, boundaries, personal space, and so on, the survivor should not hesitate to look for another caregiver.

In addition to the issue of collective denial, another alarming area is that of helping professionals who sexually abuse their clients. More and more, details of the sexual abuse of clients by psychotherapists, physicians, sex therapists, and other human service professionals are coming to light. Incest survivors seem to be more at risk than most women to become further victimized by their caregiving professionals. If someone with a professional relationship suggests that boundaries be crossed, the survivor should beware. For instance, a therapist who suggests dinner together, a movie together, a sexual encounter together is breaking therapist–client boundaries. Since incest survivors have a long history of people violating their boundaries, this is extremely dangerous and the therapist is acting unethically. The survivor needs to terminate the relationship and should seriously consider reporting the caregiver to authorities. For more information on therapists' sexual abuse of clients, read *Sex in the Therapy Hour* (1989) by Carolyn M. Bates and Annette M. Brodsky.

As concerned adults, women can do things to break through collective denial and the sexual abuse of women by professionals. People have been organizing to educate school personnel about the effects of sexual abuse, the signs of abuse, the actions that must be taken if abuse is suspected. In a small community in upstate New York, several incest survivors, helping professionals, and concerned citizens formed a group called the Independent Sexual Abuse Watch (I SAW). This group sponsored an incest speakout to which social services personnel, school personnel, court officials, police agents, and the general community were invited. It included talks by therapists, legal experts, and incest survivors as a means of educating the public. This project was started by seven women.

In Boston, there is the Boston Alliance to Stop Abuse by Therapists (BASTA). This advocacy group has taken on the task of warning potential victims of therapist abuse, providing training and support groups for women who have been abused by their therapists, and educating both professionals and others about what constitutes client abuse.

The work of childhood sexual abuse survivors and other concerned women has begun to have an impact on professional malpractice as it relates to protecting women and children. This work has often been an outgrowth of the incest recovery process, in which a survivor's mission catapults someone to the forefront of advocacy work. Because of the work of survivors, there are children who are now being protected from abusive families. There are women who are being protected from abusive therapists. There are systems that formerly turned their backs on abused children that are now actively pursuing child safety in the home.

Within the last year, I have been both disheartened and heartened by interactions I have had with school personnel. On one occasion, I was told by several different teachers in a school district that they were discouraged from interceding in cases where they suspected child abuse. They were told that it caused too many problems and put their school in jeopardy from parents who would make trouble for the school district. There was a fear of lawsuits and accusations of false reporting.

Yet on another occasion I was invited to speak to a school district on children at risk. It was explained to me by the principal that teachers requested more information on child abuse so that they could take a more active role in protecting their students. The school administration supported this position and arranged for several in-service trainings on this subject.

Based on these and other interactions, I recognize that progress in the field of child abuse prevention is being made, yet there is still a long, long way to go before children's tales of sexual violence and abuse will be acknowledged. However, I am still optimistic, and I believe that women can make a difference; they can break through the obstacles that keep women and children at risk.

Margaret, in explaining her recovery process, touched on her desire to make a difference for others: "I am proud of myself. I have opportunities to abuse my kid, but I don't and I won't. . . . One of my goals is to do what I can do so no other children have to deal with this. I need to make sure that this never happens to my kid."

The work of such women as Margaret is making a difference. Women are confronting collective denial and forcing communities to look at issues that have previously been ignored.

CHAPTER SEVEN

Ending the Burden of Secrecy

Carrying the weight of the secret from childhood into adulthood is burdensome and oppressive. Even when the adult is not consciously aware that she was sexually victimized as a child, the weight of the secret continues to affect all aspects of her life. Some childhood secrets, such as surprises or impish gossip, are fun. A childhood secret of sexual abuse imposed by a powerful adult is frightening and heavy. While having a secret might initially be exciting, it soon becomes burdensome and when left untold becomes more and more difficult to disclose.

Sometimes self-disclosure can be the most difficult task. Initially, if the survivor has memory of what was in fact incest, she may view it as appropriate adult–child interaction that she is just misinterpreting. "All fathers wrestle with their daughters and I'm just overreacting to the fact that his penis was always slipping out from his pajamas/underwear/bathing suit/robe/etc." Or "My uncle was a creative photographer, that's why he was always taking pictures of me in the nude." Or "I don't remember wetting the bed at other times, but I'm sure my grandfather was right when he would push me away from his lap and tell me that I wet the bed again." Sometimes when survivors have memory of abuse, they cannot even get to the point of thinking about the details and finding an explanation as in the examples above. When a memory begins to surface, they just push it away.

When a survivor has no memory of the sexual abuse, she often has signs that *something* traumatic occurred during childhood. Even though she is without concrete memory, she feels the weight of the secret she carries and lives a life in which the effects of childhood sexual abuse are present. Perhaps she has difficulty with intimacy and sabotages her relationships. She may have difficulty with sexual relationships. She may drink and use drugs to escape her pain. She may have bouts of serious depression. She may be bulimic or anorexic. She may be a compulsive eater who uses food and body size to protect herself from feelings of powerlessness. Without concrete memories, she has no explanation for her behavior, yet she is affected by the burden of the childhood sexual abuse. And although denial continues to protect her from facing her childhood trauma, she may begin to admit to herself that *something* happened to her during her childhood that is affecting her current life. Memory is not needed for a survivor to begin the acknowledgment process.

In the beginning stages of acknowledgment, the survivor admits that something *may* have happened to her. This is a first, yet very big, step. This admission is usually followed by a renewed denial, and a period in which the survivor vacillates between the belief that "something may have happened" and the belief that "nothing happened; I am making this all up." This is a common experience, and as the acknowledgment and later disclosure process continues, the survivor will vacillate less and less and ultimately come to believe that the incest did in fact occur.

The initial acknowledgment and later tentative self-disclosure usually follows an event that sparks the recovery process. As mentioned previously, this event is often referred to as the "trigger point." For a survivor who may or may not have some memory of the childhood sexual abuse, a trigger point can be just about anything that stimulates memories. The most common trigger points are the death of the perpetrator, the birth of the survivor's baby, the survivor's child reaching the age at which the survivor was abused, the survivor's child being sexually abused, or reading, hearing, or seeing a story about sexual abuse. Veronica, while watching the made-for-television movie about incest, *Something About Amelia,* said, "That happened to me." Her husband said, "What?" And Veronica immediately recanted and said, "I didn't say anything." She later told me that at that moment she had her first realization that she was an incest survivor. She was not ready to admit it to herself, let alone another human being, so she quickly pulled back from her first spontaneous admission. Years later, she and her husband would point to that evening as the turning point in her life and recovery process.

For a survivor who has no memory of the abuse, the initial cautious admission that something *may* have happened often occurs because she begins to look at signs that her life is not working for her in a way that she would like. Although the signs may have always been there, it generally takes a particular event for the survivor to begin actively examining how she operates in the world. After I gave a guest lecture on incest to a college class, a young woman approached me after class and began to cry. She told me that although she didn't remember anything happening to her as a child, she felt as if I were describing her in my talk. Eventually this woman entered into therapy with me. I soon learned that she not only had no memory of anything traumatic happening to her as a child, she had no memory of her childhood at all—a common phenomenon for incest survivors. However, she exhibited clear signs of having been sexually abused as a child. As a young adult, she was depressed. She became involved with abusive men who were considerably older than she. She had difficulty forming relationships and was usually isolated and alone. She was a compulsive eater who used food as a companion. She often felt hopeless and suicidal.

The individual signs by themselves may not necessarily indicate a history of childhood sexual abuse, but together they paint a picture of an adult survivor. No memory of her childhood occurred to protect her from facing events that were too traumatic. She was severely depressed because although she had no memory of the abuse, she had the effects of abuse and the understandable response to being powerless and vulnerable. When she became involved with older, abusive men, she was replicating the familiar relationship that she had had with her father. Her difficulty in forming relationships resulted from her protective response to her childhood—being distrustful and distant. Her compulsive eating not only helped her take care of herself in the only safe way she knew how—by feeding herself—but also gave her a large body that could help her not feel small, childlike, and vulnerable.

After several months in therapy, she began to explore her relationship with her family, particularly her father. She began to reclaim some childhood memories, memories that further confirmed sexual abuse. These memories included changing, at about age eight, from a shy, docile girl to a hostile, aggressive "troublemaker," being sexually active at age nine and performing oral sex with a neighborhood boy without any coaching or instructions, an incident during the same year when she was scolded and pushed away by her mother for attempting to french kiss her goodnight, and having a sexual relationship with a teacher in high school (which was a concrete example of her being sexually abused as an adolescent). She also remembered having a close relationship with her father as a child and it becoming strained around early adolescence.

Age eight or nine seemed to be the turning point in this client's life. So she and I began to concentrate on those years. Our work included, among other interventions, her writing a letter to her father from her eight-year-old self. She had much difficulty doing this and said she couldn't do it on her own. So we set up my office as she remembered her bedroom as a child, including the scattering of dolls and stuffed animals throughout the room. I gave her a crayon and some paper, with the instructions to divide the paper in half. The left side of the paper was for the letter to her father from her eight-year-old self. On the right side I asked her to write the intrusive thoughts that were stopping her from writing the letter, such as, "this is stupid" or "I can't do this." She was given about twenty minutes in which to write (more time can be allotted for this exercise, but in this case I wanted to leave time for her to read to me what she wrote and for us to process the activity). Two chairs were set up for her to use as she read what she wrote. One was for the eight-year-old; the other chair was for the adult who was running interference for the little girl. The client completed the exercise, read what she wrote, and had a dialogue between her little girl and her adult. She began to see how she, as an adult, was protecting herself from knowing herself as the sexually abused child that she had been.

This client has not yet completely accepted the fact that she was sexually abused as a child, but she has reached the beginning stages of self-disclosure. She is alternating between thinking that she "*may* have been sexually abused as a child" and thinking that she is "making this all up." However, in spite of going back and forth, she is feeling more solid with the belief that something did indeed happen, and she is reclaiming more and more childhood memories and gaining more evidence that she was sexually abused. (Specific interventions about reclaiming memories are included in chapter 8).

The case described above is an example of someone without specific memories entering the disclosure stage. It also demonstrates the beginning of the movement from "telling myself" to "telling another." Often these steps are very close—a woman begins to tell herself that she is an incest survivor while she explores that possibility with another person. There is a difference between these steps though. Telling another may help facilitate the "telling myself" stage, but disclosure to someone else is a profoundly frightening step for the survivor to take. She may for a time feel immobilized by fear. She has carried the burden of the incest secret because the perpetrator warned her of the dire consequences of telling, and those warnings are as threatening and terrifying to the adult survivor as they were to the child she once was. In identifying the phenomenon of post traumatic stress disorder among incest survivors, we find that for them time stopped at the moment of trauma. Often this is the time at which all memory of childhood stopped. Thus, startle reactions, flashbacks, and sleep disorders, such as nightmares, occur, replicating the experience as if it were happening at that moment. Time was frozen. The survivor feels the same fears and terror as if she were a child. I remember a woman in one of my incest survivor groups who would look to the heavens with trepidation as she talked about her brother sexually abusing her. She would say, "My mother will strike me down for saying anything bad about my brother." Although her mother had been dead for ten years, she still wielded the same power that she had when my client was a little girl. Her mother was very emotionally abusive to her daughter and idolized her son who had incested her daughter. When my client trembled at the thought of her mother overhearing what she was saying about the prized son, she was responding as if she were that little girl. How could one not be petrified of telling another about this secret when in fact, for the survivor, the earth had stood still at the moment of the trauma? She was attempting to break silence as an adult with the emotional resources of a young child. Yet it is the very process of telling the secret to another that unleashes the ability to activate the adult resources to move on through the healing process. This is a very, very scary process, but it is vital in relieving the burden of the secret.

"Telling another" starts with the whisper, "I think I may have been sexually abused as a child." It is my belief that it must continue through the process of telling another person the details of the abuse. Many women have disclosed the reality that they are incest survivors without explaining in detail what they remember. To tell in detail is extremely difficult but, I believe, very necessary. To tell someone else, as well as yourself, the explicit details of this violation explodes the secret, makes it less toxic, shifts the blame and guilt from the survivor to the perpetrator, and normalizes the survivor's understanding of her childhood, her childhood coping methods, and her adult survival skills.

However, the survivor's readiness level is extremely important. She must be ready to disclose in detail. She must find the disclosure vehicle that feels safest to her—written form, art form, verbalization, and so on—and her disclosure must be met with empathy and support, not shock and disapproval. To force the disclosure process can be as abusive and damaging as the original sexual abuse itself. Therefore, it is important to honor the fact that incest survivors are the experts on their condition. They are in charge of their healing process. As a therapist, I introduce the idea that at some time the survivor may benefit from telling of the incestuous abuse in detail, but that she is the one who will make the decision about when to do so. I do not introduce this idea in the beginning of our therapeutic work, but later, after she has been actively working with me on the incest healing process. When she chooses to disclose in that way, my job is to bear witness and to support her.

When the survivor begins to disclose in detail, even though she is ready, she may go into a major crisis. She may regress to old behaviors and emotions, or she may feel overwhelmed with new and old emotions. She may need around-the-clock support. She may need to be in touch with her support system in a more regular way. She will need to be reassured that this will pass and that things will get better, and she needs to be reminded of her strengths and the good work she has already accomplished. And these assurances and reminders are all true. This stage will pass, and she will become stronger, and she will become more empowered as she continues to move through the incest recovery process. Disclosure will facilitate her passage. She will move beyond the whisper of "I think I am an incest victim," through the painful details of her incest history, through the louder voice that states, "I am an incest survivor," to the integration of the incest into the larger picture of whom she has become—a woman, a lover, a partner, a mother, a worker, an activist, whatever she has become and continues to become. This process starts with self-disclosure and it continues with unburdening oneself of the secret by telling someone else. The process is scary. Therefore it is important that the survivor takes small, careful steps along the way. She may need to try out telling someone by perhaps writing in a journal, talking to a mirror, explaining it to her pet, or finding that one trusted person who can accept her and support her no matter what she says or does. It is important to notice with these smaller steps of disclosure that the earth is still standing after each one.

Disclosure to oneself and to another are necessary steps in the healing process. Disclosure to family members or confrontation of the perpetrator(s), though not necessary, may be helpful. However, the survivor's emotional and physical safety are imperative and must be considered first. If she feels that her safety will be compromised by disclosing to a particular person who may not be safe, she must defer to safety. She must disclose to someone; she does not have to disclose to everyone. As mentioned previously, we do a disservice to incest survivors by implying that confrontation is a necessary step for healing. Confrontation and family disclosures may be helpful in that they change the dynamics of the family, but if such choices are potentially harmful to the survivor, the survivor's need to protect herself from further trauma is overriding. Therapists, partners, and friends must support the survivor in her choices around confrontation and disclosures. There is no right or wrong in this area, except that emotional and physical safety are essential and that the survivor must assess and reassess for herself what will help the healing process to continue.

CHAPTER EIGHT

Recovering Memories

Many incest survivors have little or no memory of the childhood sexual abuse they suffered. Many survivors have little or no memory of any portion of their childhood. Yet incest survivors are entitled to their histories. Just as African-Americans have been denied their history through the dismantling of their culture, their language, and their heroes and heroines, and just as women have been denied their history by their exclusion from the written recordings of time, the demeaning of their contributions to the culture, and their invisibility in society other than as sexual objects, incest survivors are denied their personal history when childhood events are not accessible. We know the effects of lost and stolen history—the loss of a sense of self, tattered self-esteem, an uncertainty about reality, a denial of self-worth. To deny someone her or his history is another form of abuse.

It is important for incest survivors to reclaim their histories no matter how painful the process may be. Often during incest recovery work, the survivor is flooded with memories. This can be a traumatic time, yet it is also an empowering time in which the survivor begins to feel validated for her beliefs, emotions, actions, and reactions. Survivors who do not have specific memories often have gnawing doubts about what they know to be true. Memories are important yet are often inaccessible to the survivor.

There are generally two reasons why a survivor may not have memories of the sexual abuse. The sexual abuse may have taken place during a preverbal, precognitive stage. The child may not have had the words or thoughts to understand what was happening to her. For instance, an infant cannot discriminate between sucking on a pacifier and sucking on a penis. If she were forced to suck on a penis as an infant, the survivor may not have the specific memory, but she lives with the effects of the sexual abuse. She may not have visual memories but instead sensory or physical memories; memories that are stored as emotional responses in her body. She may experience the memory of it as fear, discomfort, choking, or other kinds of pain. As an adult without memory of sexual abuse, she may experience panic attacks and gagging when engaging in oral sex. Another infant may have had her clitoris stroked as a bedtime ritual. As an adult she may have no specific memory of this, yet while being sexual with her partner, at the moment of orgasm she may begin to weep uncontrollably. In therapy, as in life, these women may have a sense that they were sexually abused as children, but they may have no access to their memories, and they may never have access to these traumatic events. Although I have worked with women who have regained memory of the sexual abuse that occurred when they were toddlers and infants, in my experience instances of regaining such memories are rare. In cases where specific memory is not retrievable, sexual abuse can be validated by sense memories, childhood coping skills, childhood and adulthood behavior patterns, and acquired survival skills. Sometimes it can be validated by friends and family members who knew the survivor and her family during those earlier times.

Another common reason for a lack of memory is the psyche's ability to protect one from trauma. Incest is traumatic, and many times the defense mechanism of denial protects us from being overloaded with pain. When a survivor has no memory of the abuse because she is protecting herself, she will have no memory until she is able to bear what initially was unbearable. Like the survivor who has no memory because she was too young to remember, she often has signs that she was sexually abused as a child. It is often these signs that prompt her to begin to look at the possibility that she is an incest survivor. When a woman has little or no memory of her childhood whatsoever, it can be a sign that something traumatic occurred during her childhood. The trauma is not always incest, but when lack of memory is joined with other signs, problems with intimacy and/or sex, hypervigilance, repeated victimization, mistrust of one's perceptions, depression, self-destructive behavior, compulsions and addictions, and so forth, it points to childhood sexual abuse.

One does not have to lose total memory of one's childhood in order to have lost the memory of specific acts of childhood sexual abuse. These memories have been repressed because they are too traumatic. However, memory that has been lost to this repression can be recovered. It may return in tiny pieces or come back as a flood. The survivor may fluctuate between times of tremendous recall and times with little recall—there is no set pattern of how one reclaims childhood memories. What is important to understand is that we remember what it is helpful for us to remember. Therefore as terrifying and distressing as memories may be, we will only remember what we are able to bear.

Being too young at the time of the abuse to remember it and being too traumatized to remember it seem to be the most common reasons for childhood amnesia. There are, however, other causes of childhood events being inaccessible to the survivor. If the sexual abuse occurred only once, it may have blurred in with other childhood events. If the sexual abuse occurred frequently, it may be difficult to distinguish between the different sexual events, and they may all blur together without specific times and actions being particularly noteworthy. If the sexual abuse was one aspect of an abusive childhood that included emotional and physical, as well as sexual, violence, it may have gone to the background as other traumatic memories emerged.

One does not need memory to heal from sexual abuse. However, many survivors wish to remember details so that they can better understand their life patterns and so that they can validate concretely what they know intuitively. Memories will come when and if they will be helpful. What is most important for the survivor to remember is that she does not need memories to know she was sexually violated as a child. Although she may wish to remember details, she does not need *proof* that sexual abuse took place. She is not on trial, even if perpetrators, family members, or friends attempt to put her on the defensive.

Memories come in different forms. Flashbacks are memories that occur when the survivor relives an event. This may occur at any time, but usually follows a trigger point, such as a certain smell, color, touch, noise, or act. Often the survivor does not recall the catalyst for the flashback.

Flashbacks are often visual, but they may also occur through the other senses. Some women have *emotional flashbacks* in which they reexperience an overwhelming emotion as if the sexual abuse were occurring again. These may be different from literal flashbacks, in that the survivor may not know she is experiencing a flashback at all. She may be driving in her car and for no obvious reason suddenly be overcome with grief. She may experience that grief with the intensity she felt during the time of the sexual violence. She may or may not discover that there was a catalyst for that emotion—something that triggered her response to the incest as if she were being abused right at that moment.

Betty recalled, "I was walking in the supermarket—my basket full of groceries—and for what seemed like no apparent reason, I couldn't breathe. I felt a tightness in my chest. I had to flee. I left my cart in the aisle and ran to my car. After a few minutes in the car, I began to calm down."

Flashbacks can be extremely frightening and debilitating, yet they are a way the survivor can access memory, for if she is not emotionally paralyzed by the intensity of the flashback, she can record and use the flashback as a way of going deeper into childhood memory. Some survivors have reported deliberately staying with the flashback to see what memories emerge. Often survivors are able to do this by using childhood coping methods, such as detaching from the event, to witness the flashback as an objective recorder. At a later time, in the presence of a trusted support person, the survivor can relive the flashback with congruent affect and gain access to further events of her childhood.

Sometimes survivors are overwhelmed with emotion because of a flashback and feel as if they cannot escape the terror of the abuse. These flashbacks are debilitating, but they can be used later when the survivor feels safer and more in control. I remind my clients that they have lived through the worst—the actual childhood sexual abuse— and that flashbacks, although they feel as if they are the actual events, are ways that our mind allows us access to our past. Flashbacks occur because the survivor is ready to deal with the memories of her abuse. I also validate my clients' experiences of the difficulty and scariness of being flooded with memories, especially when it seems as if memories have chosen to emerge rather than that the survivor has chosen to access them. I remind my clients that they need to rev up their support networks and create safe places to which they can retreat when emotions and memories seem unbearable.

After several months of work in therapy, Rachel, age forty, had a visual flashback while making love with her husband. When she looked in her husband's face, instead of him she saw her father staring back at her. When this had happened before, Rachel would close her eyes so she saw neither her father's face nor her husband's. One night she made a conscious effort to stay with the flashback, reminding herself that she was having a visual flashback and that if it became too traumatic, she could resort to her coping skills—detaching and closing her eyes. In our next session, Rachel described the flashback and the circumstances that surrounded it. While recounting this, Rachel utilized her coping skills in our session. She looked away from me and focused on a blank section of the wall, using the wall as if it were a movie screen; in an almost trance-like manner, she then proceeded to describe the flashback. As she described the details, she regressed. She became that little girl whose father was touching her in his bed. As she relived the events, she began to cry and said, "I didn't wet the bed, Daddy." As soon as she spoke those words, she again detached and began focusing on the "movie screen" she created for herself. She sat in silence with a dazed look on her face. I softly asked her questions that would help her come back to the present, such as, "Do you know where you are now?" "How old are you now?" "Do you know who I am?" I also reminded her to focus on her breathing. I asked her to describe her body cues—did she feel a tightness in her neck, shoulders, back; did she feel upsetness or nausea in her stomach; what feelings did she feel within her body? Additionally I pointed out the coping skills I saw her using while retelling and later reliving the flashback. Because of the emotional impact of this flashback and the new memory obtained from it, I not only utilized the session for our work, I gave her an opportunity to sit quietly before leaving my office, and set up a specific time for her to check in with me later that day. She arrived at the agreed-upon time to let me know that she was "okay" and that she had arranged to be with a supportive friend for the remainder of the day. This powerful session was a catalyst for the recovery of memory. She was assured that the new memory was a sign that she was ready to continue with her recovery process. It was a sign that she was stronger and better able to take on her older, less powerful father.

Nightmares are another way of regaining memory. Nightmares may be explicit accounts of the sexual abuse that occurred during childhood, or they may consist of obscure symbols of the sexual abuse. In either case, they are frightening and disturbing, but they can be used to gain insight into one's childhood. I suggest that my clients keep a notepad by their beds so they can record dreams, including disturbing dreams. Sometimes writing down the nightmare immediately after it occurs can help the survivor return to a more peaceful sleep with the memory recorded on paper to be used at a later time. With the dream registered, the survivor has access to it and can tell it to another person. Often in therapy a client will tell me of a dream, and we will use it to go deeper into the recovery process. This may occur by the simple telling of the dream, or it may occur because of the specific dream work that we do in the session. Most often, we use dreams as a means of understanding the survivor's current state in relationship to the abuse, by having the client reenact the dream through dialogue among different aspects of it. For instance, if there was a cart with large bars in it in her dream, I would ask her to become the cart and to have a dialogue with the bars. What generally emerges is a dialogue between the symbols that relate to what is most pressing on her mind. For instance, the dialogue may result in her identifying issues of isolation and having bars that keep others out, and as a result the client may gain an insight that she can use in her life in general and in her incest healing work in particular. Through dream work the client gains access not only to memory but also to the wonderful insights and solutions she carries within her.

Whether the survivor is involved in specific dream work or not, it is important that she record her nightmares and share them with another person. It is also important for her to let the listener know what she or he needs to do to be helpful while listening to the account of the dream. For instance, if the survivor knows what would be helpful, she might say, "Don't say anything, just listen," or "Please hold me while I tell you this," or "Tell me what you make of this dream."

Nightmares can provide not only access to concrete memories and wonderful insights, but also the resolution of feelings. When gaining specific memories, the survivor may gain access to the feelings that accompany them. One woman, Candace, described a recurring nightmare that she used to work through her anger:

> Everyone in my family was in my mother's living room. I came in dressed in very loose tai chi clothes, and I had a weapon that I was holding in both my hands. I could never clearly see it—like a sword—but it wasn't with substance. And I massacred my family and I danced around them. And in my dream the walls were literally dripping. There was nothing recognizable there, and I didn't have a drop on me—not a drop. Blood and gore, but not a drop on me. There wasn't a recognizable piece of them left, and I didn't have a drop on me. The first time I had the dream, I was afraid that I'd really take that anger and rage and really do that. The second time I had the dream, it helped validate the rage I had and helped me say, "Yup, that's what I feel, and I

have every reason to feel that way." And the third time I had it, it was like, "Well wasn't that fun, I've killed off my family, and I've taken care of that." I let myself enjoy resolving the anger and rage. The first time I was terrified, the second time I was afraid, and the third time I was smacking my lips.

Candace sees the dream as a turning point in the resolution of her feelings toward her family and is in fact able now to resume a relationship with them.

Flashbacks and nightmares are ways in which memories and feelings emerge without the conscious effort of the survivor. They seem to appear out of nowhere. If they can be put into their proper perspective and understood as memories and not actual threats to the survivor, they can be used constructively in the incest recovery process.

Survivors can consciously work on accessing memories. One of the most effective ways of regaining memories is by actively giving up addictions and compulsions. Alcohol, drugs, food, sex, and buying gadgets are ways to repress memories and feelings. When uncomfortable or disturbing feelings emerge, the survivor may run to the refrigerator, run to the liquor cabinet, run to the bedroom, or run to the shopping mall. These are ways we distance ourselves from our pain, but to actively reclaim memories it is important to eliminate these addictive, compulsive behaviors. Survivors can get help in working through these counterproductive behaviors. Twelve-step programs, such as Alcoholics Anonymous, Adult Children of Alcoholics, Gamblers Anonymous, and Narcotics Anonymous, may be resources for overcoming these addictions. In addition, residential rehabilitation may be necessary. Involvement in specific addiction/compulsion recovery therapy is also helpful. Issues around compulsive eating can be addressed through various means; I often recommend support groups and therapy work modeled after the strategies for dealing with food issues presented in Geneen Roth's *Breaking Free From Compulsive Eating* and Jane Hirschmann's and Carol Munter's *Overcoming Overeating*. (Resources on addiction and compulsive eating are listed in the bibliography.)

Once feelings are not stuffed down via alcohol, drugs, food, shopping, or sex, the survivor can begin to work through her feelings and begin to recognize the body cues for different emotions. As emotions emerge, memories soon follow. It is important that the survivor utilize her support network, including therapy, to understand her feelings and to accept them as appropriate responses to life experiences. It is also important that the survivor create a safe place for herself. This may be a special room, a serene spot, a relaxation technique, a supportive environment. She may need solitude, or she may need to be with others.

Controlled regression is another means of recovering memory. This is a way to go back to earlier times and reexperience particular events and emotions; with the guidance of a trained therapist, the survivor can relive childhood traumas. The survivor must have much support and comfort during and after this process, and it is important that controlled regression take place with a trusted and trustworthy person who can guide the survivor past the trauma to a safer place, a place in which she knows she is protected from abuse and violence.

Family albums and pictures from childhood are also useful. I know of many survivors who have not looked at family pictures since leaving their childhood residences. I often ask clients to bring childhood snapshots to our sessions. At times, a certain dress or a certain car or a certain facial expression can bring back a specific memory or a flood of memories; sometimes just viewing how people in the photograph stood in relationship to each other can illustrate family dynamics that had been forgotten by the survivor.

Writing exercises can be very helpful in reclaiming memory. I suggest that all my clients maintain journals. The journal may be used for free writing or for responses to specific exercises that I suggest. I may ask the client to write a letter to an imaginary child who is currently being sexually abused. This letter of comfort, support, and suggestions may trigger a memory from the survivor's own childhood. I may ask another client to write a description of her life at age ten as she imagines it might have been. This, too, may trigger a memory. I may ask a client to spend an hour writing in her journal anything that comes up without monitoring or censoring what she writes. This exercise may be a catalyst for memories. *Courage To Heal,* by Ellen Bass and Laura Davis, has specific writing exercises that may be helpful for a survivor in recovering memories.

Sometimes I suggest to a client that she try to recreate her childhood space. If she does not recall what her room was like, I suggest that she just create a childhood space from her imagination. This may be done in my office, at her home, at the home of a friend. Where it is done is less important than having the opportunity to reflect back and allow whatever emerges to emerge.

Other forms of creative work may be catalysts for remembering one's childhood and its traumas. Painting, sculpting, dancing, and psychodrama have often been effective ways to reclaim memory, particularly memories that have not been recorded by the logical, verbal part of the brain. Through creativity one can regain sensory memory.

Memories of sexual abuse have been stimulated by the emergence in the 1970s of incest survivors' writings, and in the 1980s of media coverage of incest in the form of movies, television programs, documentaries, newspaper and magazine articles. Bibliotherapy, including incest survivors' stories, can be very helpful, and I have an extensive library of books and videos on incest and other forms of childhood sexual abuse that I make available to my clients.

I am often asked about the use of hypnosis for the recovery of memories. Although I maintain a resource list of reputable hypnotherapists, my bias is not to use hypnosis as a way to work on the recovery of memory. Even with hypnosis, one only remembers what one is ready to remember. I believe that the survivor needs to respect her recovery process and have faith in her ability to recover memories when she needs to recover them. If she is ready to use memory in her healing, it will arise without hypnosis. However, I am aware that some survivors may want to try hypnosis, and if they do I will support their decision.

Some survivors experience the emergence of memories from a detached, removed perspective. They view memories as if they are stories, or movies, or slides that are passing on a screen. Others reclaim memories as if reliving the childhood trauma—they can feel the emotions and express the pain, grief, anger, rage, and sadness that accompany the memories. However memories emerge, they need to be respected and used to help validate the survivor's perceptions and life experiences. Some of the incest recovery literature emphasizes the need for survivors to remember and tell their stories with the "appropriate" affect, meaning that they should tell their stories with feelings of sadness, hurt, anger, and so forth. Although it can be very helpful to have feelings accompany memory, we do a disservice to incest survivors to insist upon a "correct" way to work through memories. There is no right or wrong way to reclaim memories; how ever memories surface, they need to be attended to and honored as a means of continuing the incest recovery process. As already noted, when memories will be helpful to the survivor, they will surface. When intense emotions need to accompany the memories, they, too, will arise.

Sometimes with the onset of memory, the survivor is flooded with images and thoughts of the chilhood abuse. It's as if she cannot stop thinking about it, even at the cost of her ability to work, to play, to interact with others. She may find herself unable to push these flashbacks and thoughts away. When one of my clients experienced the onset of new memory, it was as if a floodgate had opened. She found that she was so preoccupied with the sexual abuse that she could not perform simple everyday tasks. She came to our therapy session and told me that she kept trying to push these thoughts away but it was just not working. I pointed out to her that this flood of memories was a way in which her psyche was letting her know that she was ready to look at the abuse and that as she tried to push them away they kept creeping into her daily thoughts as a way of demanding that she attend to them. I gave her the analogy of an attention-seeking child who does all sorts of things so she or he will be noticed. The more one tries to ignore the child, the more demanding the child becomes. When the child is attended to in a positive way, the child's demands usually diminish. I thought that her attempts at avoiding her new memory might be the reason for its intrusion into her life when she least wanted it. I recommended that she make a commitment to set aside time each day to attend to her memory of the sexual abuse. Attending to it might include spending a period of time writing about the abuse or thinking about the abuse or reading about sexual abuse or creating rituals about abuse—any way that she felt comfortable giving attention to her sexual abuse history. After deciding to spend a half-hour daily writing in her journal about her memories, she told me that the memory no longer was interfering with her work and play. She was now working on the incest recovery rather than having the incest memory work on her.

It is important that incest survivors create for themselves ways to reclaim memory that do not replicate the sexual abuse. This can be done by creating a safety network that will provide support for the emotions that arise with the onset of memory. Without this network, survivors run the risk of being flooded with pain that may seem like a replication of the childhood sexual abuse.

This supportive network may include a therapist, friends, other survivors, allies within the family, and so forth. The survivor also needs a safe space, a place that is designed to provide protection and security. Relaxation tapes may be helpful. Other forms of relaxation may be necessary, such as massage, biofeedback, deep breathing techniques, and yoga. I have often involved clients in guided imagery, an exercise that includes deep relaxation and peaceful imagery that lets the client feel tranquil and secure. This guided imagery can be conjured up when she needs respite from disturbing emotions and body reactions. Mostly, the survivor needs to make her needs her priority. She must take care of herself, including eliminating self-destructive behaviors and addictions, resting, exercising, eating in sync with her body's needs, and responding to her needs for comfort and safety. If a safe, loving environment is created, this can be the place to which the survivor can retreat when dealing with the pain and fear that occurs during the emergence of memory. This can be the place for her to take sanctuary from the aspects of her healing process that are most painful.

CHAPTER NINE

Feelings

Emotions are often the most talked-about aspect of human development, yet they are often the most misunderstood. It has been said by some that having emotions is one way in which human beings are distinguished from other members of the animal kingdom, yet we know more about other aspects of ourselves than we do about this one. Evidence in a recent study suggests that certain emotional responses occur before the brain actually registers what is causing the reaction; in other words, the emotion occurs before thought: We *feel* before we *know*, which may explain in part why some of our emotions are so frightening and difficult for us to understand (Goleman, 1989). Psychology and other human service fields are engaged in understanding human emotions and helping clients to "work through" emotions as a means of self-actualization. Yet it is the powerfulness of emotions that may wreak havoc on an incest survivor's ability to face the incest recovery process head on. Often when a survivor begins to actively work on her incest recovery process, she is overcome with emotions and wants to somehow put the process away and make those feelings go away. However, not only is it almost impossible to stop the process once it has begun, it is my belief that the incest trauma was interfering with the survivor's ability to live and to love long before she took an active role in her recovery. Thus, it is better for her to be working on the incest than to have the incest working on her. And feelings are an important aspect of working on the incest recovery process.

Two of the most common ways survivors of childhood sexual abuse experience life are by being intellectual ("locked into their heads") and by being flooded with feelings ("locked into their emotions"). For instance, some survivors can tell you the details of their sexual abuse as if they were journalists reporting the news, but they have no idea how to answer the question, What are you feeling right now? One of the goals of therapy with such a survivor is to help her recognize her feelings. We might, for example, work on having her look at body cues, such as a clenched jaw or a shortness of breath, as a means of identifying possible emotions.

Other incest survivors are flooded with emotions. They can identify being sad, depressed, lethargic, anxious, enraged, and so on, but the strength of their feelings, and their absorption in them, is often incapacitating. They find it almost impossible to mobilize their resources because they are overwhelmed by their emotions. In therapy with this survivor, one of our goals will be to help her learn to understand her emotions and her emotional responses and to use her feelings and thoughts so that they serve her best interests. If it is clear that she is "stuck" and feeling incapacitated because of the intensity of her emotions, we may need to be more action-oriented than feeling-oriented in our therapy. This is not to say that feelings will be dismissed; they will be acknowledged as important, but they will be seen as catalysts for action. An eastern Zen therapy, introduced to the United States by David Reynolds and called "Constructive Living," may be helpful here (see the bibliography); it recommends that we "acknowledge the feelings and do what needs to be done"—in other words, attempt to change feelings by changing behavior. For instance, if a survivor feels isolated, rather than dwelling on how bad it feels to be isolated, she may be given an assignment to make one social connection with one other person sometime during the next two weeks. This is a small step (although for some clients, it may be a large step and may be inappropriate for an initial assignment) and the beginning of the process of building on successes that we hope will help the survivor overcome the feeling of isolation. (This approach is used only after careful assessment and work with the client and is not utilized as a matter of course.)

This discussion is meant not to challenge the reader to work with incest recovery issues in certain ways, but rather to illustrate that the issue of emotions can be manifested in two distinct ways. The first way, being locked into one's head, may interfere with the survivor's recovery process, and the survivor may need to learn how to feel. The second way, being locked into one's emotions, may also interfere with the survivor's recovery process, and the survivor may need to learn how to act. Ideally, the therapy process will have the survivor learn to honor both her head and her heart and thus be able to feel, think, and act as a means of healing from child sexual abuse.

Before looking at specific emotions and ways to work with them, I would like to put forward some generalizations. The first is that it is necessary to learn not to be afraid of feelings. This may be easier said than done. We live in a culture that attributes the affective domain to women and thus devalues it, and we have been taught to avoid "negative" emotions at all cost. Therefore we are a culture addicted to drugs, alcohol, work, money, food, and so on as means of avoiding our emotions. Even our term for emotions, *irrational,* has a pejorative meaning. Yet emotions unattended can lead to illness, incapacitation, phobias, accidents, even death, so it is essential that we learn to listen to our feelings. Feelings cannot be willed away. Feelings cannot hurt us. Our actions in response to our feelings may be detrimental to our well-being, but feelings in themselves are not bad. We are not in control of our feelings; we are in control only of our behavior. If possible, I suggest that survivors allow their feelings to surface rather than avoid them through addictions and compulsions or prescribed medication. However, if feelings are leading to self-destructive or other destructive behavior, prescribed medication may be necessary—an antidepressant drug for depression or an antianxiety drug for anxiety. The use of medication should be seen not as a failure but rather as a life-affirming alternative to suicide, self-mutilation, or abusive behavior.

The second generalization is that it is sometimes necessary to "let it bleed." I give the example of a sore that has scarred over without the necessary cleansing and therefore later becomes infected. Sometimes we must cut open the sore and let the infected blood and pus ooze. In some ways, when we have denied our feelings and have detached without experiencing the reality of our emotions, we are as if infected. Sometimes we need to emotionally let it bleed so we can rid ourselves of the infection, cleanse ourselves, and move onward in our healing. Of course, the process of letting it bleed is scary and painful, so it is necessary for survivors to utilize a support network, avoid people and situations that are not understanding or encouraging of their process, and be especially nurturing of themselves. Since survivors often do not know how to nurture themselves, learning to do so may also be a therapy goal. Having the survivor generate a list of activities and behaviors that are soothing and comforting to her is one way to help her begin to learn how to pamper herself.

Finally, I remind my clients that although there are right and wrong ways to behave, there is no right or wrong way to feel. For instance, if a woman *feels* like strangling her partner, that is okay; if she actually *does* strangle her partner, that is not okay. That might seem obvious, but I know many people who feel guilty and evil because of their thoughts and feelings. Such reactions are usually based on the faulty belief that we are in control of our emotions and thoughts and that we are in control of whether or not we feel them. To dispel this myth, I ask my client to look at an object in the room, close her eyes, and not think about that object for a prescribed amount of time. Needless to say, no matter what she does to avoid thinking about the object, her mind continues to focus on what she was told not to think about. This is a simple exercise to illustrate the point that we cannot control our thoughts and feelings and that since we can't control them, they are neither right nor wrong, neither good nor bad.

There seems to be a progression through different feelings as one works on recovering from incest. Usually beginning before the survivor actively engages in the incest healing process and continuing through the beginning stages of her recovery, the survivor feels depression, anxiety, or a combination of the two, an agitated depression. These emotions are often combined with feelings of guilt and powerlessness.

As the survivor continues her recovery from sexual abuse, she feels profound anger and rage. This powerful stage, in which she learns to express her anger in a life-affirming rather than destructive form, in turn gives way to a deep sadness and grief. The eventual goal is to let go of the debilitating emotions entirely and begin to feel some type of peace. These emotions that result from the stages of recovery and ways to promote movement through them will now be discussed more fully.

DEPRESSION

Depression is often a debilitating emotional state. It can stop people in their tracks and cause them to feel hopeless and bleak. In my work with incest survivors, I have met many women who could not recall a time in their lives when they did not feel depressed. Symptoms of depression include feelings of hopelessness, despair, doom, and profound sadness. Survivors often feel self-destructive and may feel suicidal. Often they live their lives in anticipation of disaster and catastrophe, though there is no concrete evidence to indicate that they are doomed. Behaviorally they may have no energy, they may lose interest in all activities, they may have periods of tearfulness, social withdrawal, and/or suicidal gestures. Sometimes the depression is chronic, having remained constant over long stretches of time. Other times it is situational, a particular event having been the catalyst for its onset.

Depression is more likely to be diagnosed as such in women than in men. This is probably true because in our culture men are encouraged to be aggressive and are given outlets for their anger and frustration whereas women are encouraged to be docile and are discouraged from openly expressing hostility and disappointment; thus women often respond to injustice and adversity by turning the feelings inward rather than expressing righteous anger.

Sometimes just entering psychotherapy, talking about the feelings and events in one's life and getting insight into one's life experiences, helps lift the depression. When the onset of therapy isn't enough, and the depression is so debilitating that suicide and other self-destructive behaviors are possible, hospitalization may be necessary. Sometimes medication in conjunction with therapy is enough to stabilize the survivor. In any event, once the depression becomes more manageable, the survivor can be given tools to help her work through it. I often suggest to my clients the use of affirmations, positive statements that are repeated over time and become accepted by the subconscious as true. For instance, a client may state many times daily, "I love myself unconditionally, and every day, in every way, I am becoming stronger and stronger." I ask her to say this upon arising in the morning, several times during the day and evening, and as she is falling asleep. Affirmations counteract the negative thoughts we have given ourselves through our daily self-criticisms. Since depression is tied in with feelings that one has little self-worth, building self-esteem is a necessary task in overcoming it.

In addition to affirmations, I also encourage clients to keep journals, so they can record their feelings and insights. I also suggest that they become involved in aerobic exercise, such as walking, swimming, jogging, or dance. If the survivor can become involved in group aerobic activities, she not only works on her depression through elevating her natural antidepressant, the endorphins, but also becomes less isolated. However, group aerobic activities may not be possible, and individual aerobic exercise is also quite helpful. If a survivor is starting an aerobic program, she should obtain the approval of her physician.

Sometimes it is helpful for the survivor to purchase a doll, a symbol of her inner child, to be nurtured. I suggest that she choose the doll carefully and that the process of locating the right doll be taken seriously. I have found that this search can sometimes be very uplifting. It can often be a catalyst for deep childhood emotions to surface, thus giving us grist for the mill as we work on childhood trauma. Besides being a vehicle through which the survivor can get in touch with her inner child, the child who has not been attended to, it can be the beginning of learning how to play and be childlike, something that is often difficult for survivors.

When depression begins to lift, the client may feel uneasy and not deserving of this new outlook and begin to sabotage her progress. One of my clients recently stopped taking her antidepressant medication after a short period of feeling less hopeless and more peaceful. After stopping the medication, she again became irritable and had suicidal thoughts. She told me she had stopped for several reasons: For one thing, while she was on medication people seemed to be responding to her differently; instead of sympathy and pity, she was receiving encouragement and caring, and she felt that her family and co-workers were being more pleasant and forthcoming. She realized that she was frightened by the change and the newness of this experience. Additionally, she felt that she didn't deserve to feel good. She believed that her depression was her punishment for being bad—that somehow she needed to be punished for being molested by her perpetrator.

Sometimes when the depression begins to lift, a survivor may feel euphoric and therefore experience a major letdown if she feels sadness or depression at a later point. The fact is that depression is a natural occurrence in life. It is appropriate to feel depression in response to disappointments and adversity. Survivors need to know that situational depression is normal and that to feel depressed occasionally is not a sign of going backward in the recovery process. It is ongoing depression that the survivor and her support network need to address in order to continue with her incest recovery process.

ANXIETY

Anxiety is another emotion commonly experienced by incest survivors. It often arises in combination with depression, but it can occur alone. Symptoms of anxiety include shakiness, jitteriness, an inability to relax, sweating, a pounding of the heart, shortness of breath, dizziness, light-headedness, sleeplessness, hypervigilance, difficulty in concentrating, excessive worrying, and excessive fearfulness.

Some ways of addressing anxiety are similar to the ways one can address depression—therapy, affirmations, journal writing, aerobic exercise. In addition, relaxation techniques are helpful. These may include deep breathing, guided imagery, yoga, and meditation. Involvement in the martial arts may be helpful because it combines aerobic activity with contemplative relaxation, as well as promotes self-confidence and the ability to protect oneself, things that are often very comforting to the survivor of childhood sexual abuse.

Biofeedback, in which the survivor learns to relax her body and mind through specific activities, has been reported to be helpful in managing anxiety and panic attacks.

Sometimes when the survivor's anxiety is interfering with her functioning, medication is necessary. For instance, if the survivor is in a constant state of agitation, she may be unable to sleep, work, play, or to take care of herself. If specific interventions, as mentioned above, are not alleviating the anxiety, an antianxiety drug may be necessary to allow therapy to progress. In all cases of prescribed medication, whether for depression, anxiety, or agitated depression, a psychiatric evaluation is necessary.

SHAME/GUILT

Feelings of shame are common among survivors and are often connected to feelings of guilt. Among the factors that prevent survivors from disclosing to others about their incest histories are the shame and guilt survivors often feel for having been sexually victimized. As children, survivors were often made to feel responsible for the sexual abuse. *You want this, You're enjoying this, If you tell you will be punished for this* are phrases perpetrators use to keep children in incestuous relationships. Children, like adults, have cognitive maps that help them make sense of the world. Since everything within the culture, including schools, churches, families, and media, tells children that adults are good and have children's best interests at heart and that mothers and fathers are loving and protective of children, a child who is being sexually abused must make sense of the world by adjusting her cognitive map. What results is a child thinking that she has somehow caused the abuse. This view of the incest often stays with her through adulthood, and she continues to feel guilty and ashamed for the sexual abuse. I often hear clients talk about feeling that deep inside they are filled with slime. They feel "bad," "evil," "immoral."

It is important for the survivor to know that these feelings of shame and guilt are common for survivors, and people who work with survivors must bring up issues of guilt and shame if they are not brought up by the survivor. Sometimes just the acknowledgment of these feelings will help eliminate them.

Additionally, it is important for adult survivors to understand the "cognitive map" process. When everything in the culture—from *Walton's Mountain* and *The Cosby Show* and other television shows and movies to ministers, rabbis, priests, teachers, and parents—indoctrinates children into believing that families and adult friends are good and trustworthy, the abused child, whose experience contradicts those messages, needs to make sense of the world. The only way a child can make sense of the abuse is to blame herself. It is incomprehensible to a small child that a father, mother, grandfather, grandmother, uncle, aunt, older brother, and so on could be bad or hateful or not have the child's best interest at heart. Therefore, it is understandable that the child would feel guilty and responsible for something that was not her fault.

Along with rational explanation of why guilt and shame are prevalent emotions for abused children and adult survivors, specific activities can be used to help the survivor work through these emotions. Exercises I will suggest to a client include writing a list of her strengths, writing a list of things she is most proud of, and exploring how feeling guilt and/or shame has served her and how it has hurt her. Additionally, we talk about the issues of power and control. To be responsible and guilty implies having power and control. In some cases, as bad as guilt and shame feel to the survivor, they feel better than powerlessness and vulnerability. Guilt and shame serve the purpose of protecting her from the dreadful feelings of being small and powerless. In these cases, it is necessary for the survivor to look at being powerless as a means of letting go of her guilt. Together we examine how the client was powerless as a child and therefore unable to be responsible for the perpetrator and his abuse.

FEAR

Survivors may have many fears—perhaps fear of people, closed spaces, intimacy, men. Perhaps she fears that one day she may sexually abuse a child. I have one client who is fearful of eating in restaurants because when she was a child her perpetrator threatened to poison her food.

Fear can be immobilizing, so it is important that fears be acknowledged and discussed. Many times a survivor identifies a fear but only through the exploration of early childhood events does she understand its origin. For instance, my client who was afraid to eat in restaurants had forgotten that the perpetrator, her father, had threatened to poison her food if she told of the sexual abuse. Another woman I know had an overwhelming feeling of terror when she went into a movie theater; later in therapy, she remembered being molested in a theater. Through the process of therapy itself, many women learn the origins of their fear, and sometimes with this knowledge alone the fear subsides.

If talking about the fear and its origin is not enough to overcome it, other approaches can be pursued. Desensitization, neurolinguistic programming, and cognitive therapy may be useful for addressing and managing fear. The survivor can also design ways of confronting her fear, such as developing a plan in which the catalyst for the fear is managed in gradual, specific steps. For instance, in the case of the survivor who was afraid of restaurants, she may first go to a restaurant without buying any food or drink. The next time, without ordering food, she may sit with a friend who is eating at the restaurant. Later she may go back to the restaurant with her friend and order a cup of coffee. This process could continue until she works up to sitting in the restaurant, ordering some food and beverage, and consuming it in the restaurant. This may very well be a slow process, but with support, encouragement, and a place in which to evaluate and process these steps, the fear is usually overcome.

ANGER

Anger, more than any other emotion, feels toxic for women, who are taught to be conciliatory, agreeable, passive. We are the ones who smooth things out. Women in general have fears of being perceived as castrating, man-hating, and "bitchy." Nothing seems worse than being perceived as an angry woman.

Incest survivors in particular have difficulty with anger. They are often fearful of expressing their anger because they feel that they will be out of control, so they "stuff" these feelings, lose touch with them, and instead feel depressed and/or self-destructive. This way of dealing with anger is usually a result of the role models for anger in the survivor's family of origin. More often than not in survivors' families, anger is associated with violence and being out of control. When my survivor clients and I explore how tyranny was maintained within the family (an issue that is discussed more fully in chapter 12), we see more often than not that it was maintained by out-of-control anger.

Barbara recalled her father's display of anger. "One time he had some grasshoppers, and he made me watch as he was tearing their legs off. He once was stung by a wasp and he killed it, then he proceeded to take out his knife and cut it into little pieces after it was dead."

Ellen, forty-three, described her father as a tyrant. "Feelings were scorned. My father would throw water in my face if I whined. He wanted us to be tough."

Amy, thirty-three, described her mother. "My mother had a serious alcoholic problem. . . . She was physically and emotionally abusive." Amy's role model of anger was destructive and violent.

In some cases, survivors feel anger but it is displaced anger; they strike out at the wrong people—their children, partners, spouses, friends—rather than give the anger to its proper source. They seem to be angry all the time.

Sometimes survivors are a combination of the two—they stuff their anger, and then like volcanoes they explode over a relatively minor infraction as if it were a major injustice. For instance, a woman has been treated unfairly at work, perhaps someone else took credit for something that she accomplished or she took the criticism for someone else's mistake and she doesn't express her anger. She comes home and her husband chastises her for not having his supper ready, and she doesn't express her anger. The neighbor carelessly backs his car over her prized rose bushes, and she smiles and says, "That's OK. No problem," and doesn't express her anger. Later her five-year-old son spills a glass of milk, and she responds with a barrage of ugly names and a smack across his face. Had she expressed her annoyances or anger as they were accumulating, her reaction to her son's mishap might have been more appropriate to his error.

Sometimes survivors find it easier to identify with the powerful perpetrator and be angry at themselves than to be angry at him. They are angry at the child who couldn't make it stop, who was small and helpless, or who may have felt physical pleasure from the sexual abuse. This is another example of displaced anger; the survivor feels rage for that little girl rather than for the abusive adult.

Without good role models for expressing anger appropriately, and with the discouragement of anger in women in general, it is not surprising that anger is a tough area for survivors. However, learning to identify anger and to express it effectively and appropriately is a necessary step in the recovery process.

As mentioned previously, incest survivors are often afraid that they will be out of control and may do something horrible if they ever begin to express their anger. They fear that their anger will lead to violent, uncontrollable rage. What survivors are mixing up, when they experience this fear, is the difference between an emotion and a behavior. Feeling anger is just that—a feeling. There may be physiological components—but it's still just a feeling. Being violent and destructive is a behavior. Feelings unto themselves are not right or wrong, good or bad, legitimate or illegitimate. But because of the fear of potential behavior, the survivor does not allow herself to feel the emotion.

When the survivor can understand the difference between feelings and behaviors, she has taken the first giant step toward acknowledging her anger. When I am working with a client who says she is not feeling, that she is numb, I ask her to listen to her body cues. What is happening in and with her body? How is her breathing—is it deep or shallow? How is her jaw—is it clenched or loose? How are her shoulders and neck—are they tight or loose? What's happening in her stomach? These are questions that allow her to tune into her body cues so that she can begin to identify emotions.

When she begins to identify anger, we talk about ways it can be expressed constructively and about the destructive ways anger was expressed when she was growing up. I continue to stress that anger is a powerful, empowering emotion and that physical or emotional violence is a destructive and demeaning behavior. Anger is acceptable. It is violence that is unacceptable.

In addition to validating her emotions, I am also a role model and coach for the expressing of emotions including anger and rage. I can hear the survivor's anger. I can point out when it may be misdirected. I can express my emotions when they are appropriate for our work together. I can give examples of how anger can be expressed appropriately and inappropriately. The important thing is that the survivor learn that anger is acceptable and that there are ways it can be expressed that are empowering and cathartic.

As I mentioned in chapter 4, there is an exercise on identifying the degrees of anger on a continuum from minor annoyance through varying degrees of irritation to rage. It is important to learn to distinguish between the degrees of anger and to express these emotions as they come up.

Although anger may be identified intellectually, many women have difficulty conjuring up the congruent response to this newly identified feeling. Their responses don't match the identified emotion. The survivor knows intellectually that anger is appropriate, but she may not actually feel angry. We may have to find ways to stimulate righteous anger. Often women find it easier to get angry for someone else's pain than for their own.

One way of stirring up anger is by reading childhood sexual abuse literature, such as autobiographical sketches by sexual abuse survivors. As I have mentioned, it is not uncommon for some survivors to become sexually aroused by reading such accounts, and sometimes guilt is stirred up instead of anger. Survivors must be reminded that when one's first sexual encounter was abusive, especially when the abuse was physically pleasurable, sexual violence can be erotic. The survivor has no control over this. Whether children feel pleasure or pain as a result of the sexual abuse is determined by the perpetrator. If he wants her to feel pleasure, she will feel pleasure; if he wants her to feel pain, she will feel pain. A survivor's response to stories of child sexual abuse—whether erotic arousal or anger—is often determined in childhood by the diabolical doings of the perpetrator. However, even if the survivor becomes aroused by these readings, anger is often stirred up as well, and so reading the sexual abuse literature is usually a good vehicle for this work.

Asking her to write a letter to the perpetrator can also help get the survivor to express her anger. This is done with the knowledge that it is being written as a catharsis for the survivor rather than as a vehicle to confront the perpetrator. This letter is not to be mailed; it is an outlet for pent-up anger. It is important that the survivor read this letter to a trusted friend or therapist; in addition to talking to paper, the survivor then has someone bear witness to her anger and pain.

Other ways of helping a survivor to feel her anger include writing a letter to an imaginary child who is experiencing the same abuse that the survivor experienced when she was a child; role-playing a confrontation between herself and the perpetrator; listening to other women speak of their sexual abuse at speakouts or survivor groups;

watching documentaries, movies, or television programs on child sexual abuse; and focusing on other issues that provoke anger, such as world hunger, poverty, racism—when a survivor can get angry at other areas of oppression and exploitation, connections can be made about the oppression and exploitation she experienced as a child at the hands of her perpetrator.

After anger is identified and felt, effective ways of expressing it need to be learned. There are many ways to release pent-up anger. I have found that different ways of expressing anger are helpful with different people. Some people use role-playing effectively. Others find bioenergetics techniques, such as hitting a mattress with a tennis racket, to be helpful. My clients have released their anger by ripping up newspapers, beating a large phone book with a piece of hose, screaming, breaking glass in a safe, contained environment, deep breathing, adding noises such as whimpers and animal sounds to the breathing, and writing. Outside of the therapy hour, clients have released their anger through running, physical work such as splitting wood, brisk walking, raging—a process of yelling and crying and being outraged by injustices and assaults—drumming, weight lifting, martial arts, and more. I suggest to survivors that they try anything that does not physically or emotionally hurt themselves or other people and to keep trying things until they find what works effectively for them. Driving recklessly, confronting an unstable, abusive person, putting your fist through a window, or engaging in any other behavior that is self-destructive and dangerous or that is physically or emotionally abusive to another person—these are not ways to effectively manage and release anger.

Once pent-up anger and rage are expressed and released, the survivor needs to learn to express her emotions effectively and appropriately as they occur. This needs to be done in a way that promotes her physical and emotional safety. Therefore she needs to know when and how to express anger as it occurs. *The Dance of Anger* by Harriet Goldhor Lerner (1985) is an excellent resource for women to further explore this area.

SADNESS/GRIEF

After the expression of long-pent-up righteous anger and rage about the desecration of one's childhood, profound sadness often follows. This sadness is an expression of the grief the survivor feels over her lost childhood and is not to be confused with the earlier depression. It is the mourning for a childhood that never was and a reflection of her understanding that the past cannot be willed away. This time of deep sadness may include periods of weepiness and seemingly immeasurable pain. It is a time of mourning for the family that wasn't and will never be. This stage, though it is extremely hard, is the beginning of letting go, for the survivor begins to examine the dynamics of her family and to accept the reality of her childhood rather than remain connected to a fantasy. She begins to reevaluate her family and the roles its members played in her childhood. In the case of father–daughter incest, she may begin to see her mother, for the first time, as having been powerless and her father as having been the adult responsible for the abuse. This is a often a change from the initial anger she felt toward her mother and the love and admiration she felt for the perpetrator (father).

This feeling, although it is often misinterpreted as a repeat of an earlier emotional state, is the prerequisite for letting go and making peace with the past. To get through it, the survivor should have a solid support network and a safe space to grieve; she must continue to nurture and be good to herself. This is a time for support people to reassure the survivor that what she is going through is a good and necessary process. It is a time for support people to be empathetic, to listen, to be responsive to the survivor's needs, and to reassure her that things will get better—because they will.

POSITIVE EMOTIONS

Positive emotions also emerge during the recovery process. This, too, can be very frightening. More times than not, with the emergence of positive emotions such as joy, tranquility, and powerfulness, the survivor awaits the crash. She often does not trust these positive emotions and feels that they are just the calm before the storm—which is to be expected because her childhood was filled with turmoil and crisis, and negative emotions and impending catastrophes feel familiar to her. Often I hear clients speak about "waiting for the other shoe to fall" during periods of calm.

Additionally, clients have voiced their fears about the issue of feeling powerful. As the survivor takes control of her life and takes steps to change the power dynamics in her family of origin, she may become frightened of these new feelings of power. It is important to allow the survivor to express her fears and concerns about all her emotions. It may be necessary for her support people to bring up the notion of good feelings being frightening. The survivor also needs to be reminded that there is a difference between power and control. The fact that she is feeling powerful does not mean that she will abuse this newfound power by controlling others in the way that her perpetrator controlled her.

Feelings, whether positive or negative, are just that—feelings. They need to be acknowledged and understood. Instead of immobilizing the survivor, they can be catalysts for her continued growth and recovery.

CHAPTER TEN

Sex and Intimacy

Sex and intimacy often get confused. This is particularly true for survivors of childhood sexual abuse. Sometimes survivors believe that they are having problems with sex, when in fact it is intimacy that is toxic for them. For instance, a woman may feel comfortable in a casual sexual relationship but find that she experiences sexual problems when the relationship becomes more intimate. This may be because having sex with an intimate replicates having sex with a family member. In some cases a survivor may feel that intimacy is the issue, when in fact both intimacy and sex are problems. A survivor might feel that she is unable to have intimate relationships because she cannot become physically and sexually close to anyone, when in fact she not only has issues around trust and vulnerability but also may be experiencing emotional and physical flashbacks—familiar yet frightening feelings or familiar, distressful body responses—when she tries to form a sexual relationship. She might not recognize her flashbacks as flashbacks because they are not accompanied by any visual memories. She may think instead that her turmoil is a reaction to intimacy itself.

One can confuse sex with intimacy, and one can confusedly take sex to be a requirement for intimacy. For instance, a survivor may sexualize relationships because she wants to be intimate, believing that to love and be loved by another human being requires sexual involvement. When one of the earliest intimate relationships of one's life required sex as a means of gaining attention, affection, and validation, it is not surprising that one would generalize that to all meaningful relationships. When a child's access to attention and affection is through an abusive relationship, she may see sex and nurturance as a package, and generalizing this to other relationships, she may learn, "To keep you in my life, I must succumb sexually."

Women, in general, have difficulty accepting themselves as sexual beings. We live in a culture that gives us many double messages about our sexuality. We are conditioned to believe that we must be sexually appealing but also that we must resist sexual advances. We are supposed to be sensuous and seductive but to guard our sexuality or run the risk of being deemed promiscuous. Our culture subscribes to the value of protecting girls from the sexual advances of boys and men yet expects women to look pre-pubic (e.g., without body hair) and sexually aroused (e.g., appearing orgasmic with lipstick and rouge) at all times. Girls and women are bombarded with these conflicting messages about the value of being sexually appealing to men, and being asexual in their own behavior—messages that their sexual activity defines them as either "good" or "bad," that what they do or don't do, determines whether they are "madonnas" or "whores." Given these messages, it is not surprising that women in general have difficulty acknowledging themselves to be lustful beings. To be sexual as a means of recreation, release, or lustfulness is supposed to be immoral for women. As a result, women often misinterpret lust as love, sex as intimacy. For incest survivors, these cultural messages are compounded by their learned behavior as victims of sexual abuse. In particular, when the sexual abuse was at the hands of a trusted, kindly, attentive adult rather than a sadistic, fearsome tyrant, an incest survivor learns that sex and caring relationships go hand in hand. Thus, to avoid feelings of guilt and confusion, women in general, and survivors in particular, learn to identify their sexual feelings as feelings of love and intimacy.

Although one may have issues around sex that do not relate to intimacy, and vice versa, often these issues are connected. They will be addressed separately in this chapter but are included as a package because of their connectedness. It should also be noted that the issues of sex and intimacy discussed here apply to both lesbian and heterosexual women. Special concerns for lesbians will be discussed in chapter 11.

SEX

There are several ways a survivor may relate sexually. She may be asexual, having no sexual contact with anyone, possibly including herself. She may be very sexual with numerous partners but not feel emotional or physical pleasure. She may feel obligated to be sexual within a primary committed relationship but not feel any pleasure.

She may mistake sex for intimacy and love. She may use sex to fulfill other needs, such as needs for affection, acceptance, closeness, or power.

A survivor who is asexual might view sex as dirty, a violation of her body, abusive, immoral. She might experience her body as ugly, evil, a betrayer of her integrity; she might not experience her body at all, as if she exists only from the neck up. Susan, a forty-three-year-old nun, explains about her celibacy: "I could never get my life together [enough] to get married. . . . [In the convent] I have these women who take care of some of the problems I have with sex and men, and all I have to say is, 'I'm a sister.' I didn't realize what I was doing, but it was very clever when you think about it."

Betty, age forty-four, has never had a sexual relationship other than the abusive relationship she had with her grandfather. Until very recently, she never touched her body other than in the shower. When I first suggested that she look at her body, including her breasts and her genitals, it was as if I was suggesting that she climb Mt. Everest. She was frightened, horrified, and felt totally incapable of such a feat. In addition to not touching her body, until therapy she had never even talked about her body. I suggested that she get reacquainted with her body, and we talked of the importance of reclaiming her body from her grandfather. When she made the connection, she began to realize that looking at her body and even touching her body was a healing thing to do. While at home she began to reclaim her body by looking at it, by touching it, by identifying parts of her body that she could love and admire, and by doing wonderful things for her body such as taking long, soothing baths, putting lotion on her skin, or giving herself foot massages. In time, she learned to masturbate and enjoy sexual pleasure with herself. Although she has not yet had a sexual relationship with another person, it is becoming more of a possibility for her. Because of many problems with intimacy issues—mistrust, fear, insecurity, feelings of inadequacy, lack of social skills—Betty is still not ready to interact with people whom she perceives as potential intimate and sexual partners. She continues to work on intimacy issues, and as she becomes more secure in her ability to socialize, she recognizes that a sexual, intimate relationship is within her realm of possibilities.

A survivor who is sexual with many partners without experiencing pleasure or emotional fulfillment is often a woman who is sexualizing her relationships. She does not believe that people will like her or admire her for whom she is, but rather that they will respond to her only if she can be a sexual object in their lives. She has learned from a very early age that all she is appreciated for is her ability to give sexual pleasure. Patricia, age forty-one, says, "I've always been angry at men. I think I spent a good number of years being rather promiscuous as a result of trying to conquer men. I think it gives you a guilty notion of your sexuality, when your first relationship is illicit. I had a mixed message. I was very proud of my sexuality. I was the sexy one in the family—that was a virtue, a value, a positive—but it was the only thing I thought I had going for me that could get me into a relationship."

A survivor who feels obligated to have sex within a monogamous relationship and often finds herself having sex without physical or emotional satisfaction has learned that sex is a requirement for maintaining a relationship. Additionally she has learned, as many women have, that sexual performance is a contractual agreement based on duty and obligation. There is a long-held cultural belief that women are obligated to have sex with their husbands as part of the matrimonial agreement. Until 1975 every state had a marital rape exemption based on this belief. In fact, in 1975 California State Senator Bob Wilson stated, "If you can't rape your wife, who can you rape?" (Russell, 1982) implying not only that sex is an obligation within marriage but that it can be had forcibly if necessary. An incest survivor often carries the additional burden of having been told that sex was the behavior that was required of her to prove her love for her abuser. Child victims often are told that sexual involvement is an important ingredient in loving, special relationships. They are told that sex is the cement that keeps the father–daughter/grandfather–granddaughter/uncle– niece/older friend–child relationship together, and that without it there cannot be a relationship—which for one who is small and dependent, can be an intolerable consequence. This often carries over to adult relationships in which the survivor feels obligated to have sex with her partner so that she will not threaten the relationship or break her contractual agreement.

Mistaking sex for intimacy is quite common. Survivors have learned that sex is the main thing they have to offer in a relationship, and they may see sex as the only way to demonstrate that they care for someone, or they may believe that sex is the only worthwhile thing they have to give in a relationship with someone they like. They therefore think that being sexual is being intimate.

Sometimes survivors can enjoy sex when relationships seem casual but experience sexual difficulties as a relationship becomes more intimate. The survivor may or may not feel physical and emotional pleasure during the initial stages of a relationship, but sex often becomes difficult and unrewarding as the relationship develops. Sometimes as real intimacy develops, the survivor's sexual responsiveness diminishes, and she feels as if she were replicating a sexual relationship with family. Sex as a biological need when expressed with a stranger or acquaintance feels satisfying but becomes threatening when the relationship becomes more intimate. Survivors who have satisfactory sexual relationships with lovers report that those relationships deteriorated after their marriages. They report that sex feels incestuous after the commitment ritual because their partners have become family members. In addition to the creation of what seems like an incestuous relationship, sex with a meaningful person affects specific problems with intimacy, which will be discussed later.

Sex is often used by survivors of childhood sexual abuse to fulfill other needs, such as needs for affection, attention, acceptance, or relaxation. When the survivor was a child, sex was associated with attention, caring, acceptance, love, affection, enjoyment—perpetrators often use these as rewards to the child for maintaining the sexual involvement. For instance, the perpetrator might include sex as part of a ritual incorporated into genuinely enjoyable activities such as camping, going to the movies, going for car rides, or playing games. Furthermore, perpetrators often present sex as a way of giving attention, relaxing together, being pals, and just plain having fun. As mentioned earlier, in addition to confusing enjoyment and sex, survivors commonly are confused about their roles in the sexual abuse, believing that they were somehow complicitous because the incestuous relationship seemed to give them pleasure, both physically and emotionally. Pam, age thirty-five, told how her usually distant, cold father would give her special treatment. "Dad never paid a whole lot of attention to any of us. He wouldn't play games with us. [During the sexual abuse] I felt really special. He did spend a lot of time with me riding in the car, taking me out to dinner. And the other kids didn't get that. I remember feeling very special during those times." So when Pam feels the need to relax or to get special attention, it is not surprising that sex may be the vehicle she looks to for meeting those needs.

One way Barbara escaped from the terror and fear of being sexually abused by her father was by focusing on the physical pleasure of the sex. For her, then, sex may be associated with relief from fear and anxiety and may be used to meet a need to calm down. "I think I allowed myself to get caught up with the sexual feelings as a way of escaping. . . . I could get away from the unbearable feelings of outrage and pain and injury. . . . There were times that it was sexually pleasurable or my body responded to him, and I could use those feelings as an escape from what was going on."

I work with my clients around the area of sex when they perceive it to be problematic in their lives and wish for it to change. My bias, however, is that women need to reclaim their bodies from a culture that has denigrated them and from the individuals who have abused them. Learning to receive physical and emotional pleasure via our bodies is our right, and it is a way we can reclaim our bodies. My belief is that survivors need to learn to enjoy sex and to have healthy relationships with their sexual selves, not for the sake of their partners but for their own sakes. However, I also believe that the survivor is the expert on her condition and her goals, so we work on sexuality issues if that is what she decides to do.

If a survivor wants to work on improving her relationship with sex, there are several ways that she may proceed. One way is to become celibate for a period of time—one month, three months, six months, a year, or longer. She may decide to abstain only from sex with others, or she may include abstinence from sex with herself as well. That is, she may choose to be nonsexual with others but still masturbate as a means of being sexual, or she may choose to refrain from masturbating also. Either way, in choosing celibacy the survivor is choosing to take a vacation from sex and all the issues associated with her adult sexuality. It is a way to put on hold the flashbacks that arise during sex, and it frees the survivor from being preoccupied with taking care of other people's sexual desires and needs. Celibacy may provide a welcomed respite during which the survivor can put her energies into the healing process without external or internal demands. However, this is not an option for everyone, and it is by no means the only way to begin dealing with sex and incest recovery.

One thing I do recommend is giving up obligatory sex. Sex is not an obligation, and no one needs to be sexual unless they have the desire. Desire doesn't necessarily mean sexual arousal; it can simply be the free choice to engage in a sexual activity—some survivors may choose to have sex with their partners as a means of working on sexual issues and not because they are feeling particularly aroused. The important point is that survivors must not have sex unless it's their choice. Sex with a partner out of pressure or feelings of duty restimu-lates feelings of being sexually abused. It is sex against our will, and that is abusive. A survivor who has sex with a partner out of obliga-tion does a disservice not only to herself but also to her partner and the relationship. With the continued restimulation of the abusive experience that obligatory sex entails, the survivor will not only have to work through her feelings about her childhood abuse, but she will also have new difficulties, and new associations of anxiety, fear, and abuse, with her present partner. The accumulating resentments will damage the relationship. Survivors need to reclaim sex as a means of enjoyment, connection, and intimacy rather than continue to associ-ate sex with trauma.

When working with a survivor who has decided to work on sexu-al issues without being celibate, I begin by suggesting that she and her partner agree to abstain from orgasmic sex for a period of time (one month, three months, six months, one year). This will be a time for them to learn what feels good sexually and what is sexually stimu-lating without the pressure of intercourse or other specific sexual acts that result in climax. This is a time for the survivor to learn about her body's sexual responsiveness in her own terms and without the pres-sure to perform for someone else. This is also a chance for the sur-vivor to learn to trust her partner in the areas of affection and atten-tion. Often survivors have difficulty accepting affection because they distrust their partners' motives and freeze up in anticipation of sexual overtures.

During this time of orgasm abstinence, the survivor and her part-ner might view sexually stimulating films, pictures, and videos. They might read erotic literature together and listen to erotic tapes and records. It is important that the sexual stimulus is not a re-creation of sexual abuse, that is, that it does not depict sexual violence; nor should the viewing or listening continue if one of the partners feels violated by the material. Additionally, the survivor and her partner are to explore each other's bodies in nonabusive, nurturing ways. They will agree that if any touch does not feel good or is unwanted, the specific touch will stop or perhaps the entire touch experience will stop for that time. The purpose of these exercises is to have the sur-vivor learn to enjoy sensual activities, to set limits and boundaries, and to learn to trust that her partner will not be exploitative.

It is important that the survivor and her partner agree on how they will deal with feelings of arousal. For instance, they may agree that masturbation is acceptable. One couple may decide that the partner can masturbate while the survivor holds her or him. Another couple may decide that the survivor will leave the bedroom to allow the partner to masturbate. Other couples may choose alternative ways of dealing with sexual arousal during this period of abstinence from a shared climax.

A survivor who is not with a partner, or is not wanting to be sexually involved with another person at this time, can begin to explore her own body. I suggest that this be done with the same commitment to avoid orgasm for a period of time. This is a way that the survivor can learn to enjoy her body—to learn what feels good, and to associate pleasure with more than just the release of sexual tension. Exploring one's body begins with looking at one's body, and this can be very scary for some survivors. I suggest that they look at their bodies and simply observe in a nonevaluative way. Jane Hirschmann and Carol Munter have designed in *Overcoming Overeating* an exercise to be done alone that can be very helpful for survivors who are learning to notice their bodies. They suggest that the woman stand naked in front of a full-length mirror and describe her body without judgment. For example, "I am smooth over here and rounded here and straight here and hairy here." As soon as a negative thought enters the mind, the exercise is ended until the next day; the survivor continues the exercise anew each day, until she accomplishes the goal of making it from head to toe without negative judgement.

Additionally I suggest to the survivor that she take a mirror and look at her genitals. I ask that she get familiar with her entire body as a way of making peace with the parts that have been stolen from her. Until she reclaims her body, her body still belongs to the perpetrator. Our job is to help her get it back. Sometimes the acknowledgment that the perpetrator has stolen her body and continues to have it is enough motivation for the survivor to actively work on reclaiming her body.

There are many reasons why survivors are afraid of working on sexual problems. Sex often brings up feelings of guilt, anxiety, terror, panic; and flashbacks may occur during sexual activity. However, it is because of these issues that reclaiming sex is important. It is important for survivors to work through the bad feelings they associate with sex so that they can learn to receive pleasure in ways that are fulfilling and nonexploitative. Flashbacks can be dealt with by building into the sexual act ways in which the survivor can stop the flashbacks, such as opening her eyes to see her partner, having her partner say her name, calling her partner's name, discontinuing the sexual activity, or designing key words or particular types of touch that will ground the survivor to the present. The survivor may also use the flashback as a way of regaining memory and may decide to stay with it. It is important, however, if the survivor decides to stay with the flashback, that she not restimulate emotions about the abuse that will now be linked with her present partner. Flashbacks and memories are important and can be helpful, but they can also be used in a way that is not helpful to the survivor's sexual recovery process. This issue needs to be examined carefully, and the survivor may need to discuss it with her therapist to clarify the motivation behind her decision to stay with a flashback during sex.

When a survivor seems reluctant to look at sex as an issue in her life, or states that she is asexual or has panic attacks during sex or has any other problems with sex but does not want to change, I accept her decision as correct. The survivor is the expert on her condition, and I respect her process. However, when and if she is ready to work on sexual issues, we begin specific ways of addressing them. And if a survivor is actively working on these issues but is having difficulty making changes, I may ask her four questions: What are you gaining by not changing? What pains are you avoiding by not changing? What will you gain by changing? What pain will you avoid by changing?

Recently, Karen, age thirty, was astonished to find out that she may have been resisting change in her sexual life. When I asked her to answer the four questions, she discovered that she gained time away from her husband by having panic attacks during sex. This time away from him helped her to continue to examine her sexual orientation, which had been an ongoing issue for her. Additionally, sex could continue to be the identified reason for her marital problems, and Karen could avoid looking at other marital issues. If sex became enjoyable, and her marriage was still strained, she would have to reexamine the entire relationship. The answers to the first two questions helped her to look at what she was losing by not changing: the opportunity to have a meaningful, intimate relationship with a sexual partner, and the opportunity to see if her marriage was workable. If she made peace with her sexual self, she would avoid continued isolation, loneliness, and emptiness. She would gain physical and emotional pleasure and gain knowledge about her marriage. Perhaps she would gain information about her sexual orientation. This exercise was difficult for Karen, yet it helped her to make a commitment to working on reclaiming her body and regaining her sexual self. The commitment to change is the first step and an important ingredient in the sexual healing process.

When working with survivors on sex and sexual relationships, I attempt to create an environment in which the survivor feels comfortable talking about topics that are troublesome and difficult. I suggest specific things she can do alone and with her partner. Sometimes the survivor needs to work with a sex therapist or a couples therapist in conjunction with our work. If she is to work with a sex therapist, I suggest competent, ethical therapists who have experience working with sexual abuse survivors.

In the area of sex, as in most areas, I, as a therapist, attempt to keep my bias out of the therapy hour. However, there are issues that I do address directly. When I first see a client, I specifically state that I will not hit her, harm her, or have sex with her. I say this directly, since I am aware that survivors often have problems with boundaries and often have learned to use sex as a means of pleasing someone they see as an authority. Additionally, survivors may see themselves only as sexual objects or as having only sex to offer in a relationship. Many survivors have been sexually exploited by therapists, doctors, or teachers, and therefore I wish to directly establish appropriate boundaries and clearly state my belief that sex is not part of the therapeutic alliance. I let survivors know my bias that therapists, doctors, body workers, and other helping professionals should not be sexual with their clients. Sex within the context of a helping relationship is exploitative and reenacts the survivor's childhood abuse history.

Another bias concerns sexual violence. Although I believe that sexual acts between consenting adults have no moral implications, I believe that sexual violence, such as sadomasochism, within a relationship needs to be examined carefully. Is this truly consensual behavior, or is it sexual behavior that feels familiar based on one's sexual abuse history? When working with clients who participate in sexual violence, I ask that we examine the connection between their current sexual relationship and their childhood abuse.

I am aware that many survivors of childhood sexual abuse find sexual violence to be erotic. They may be aroused by reading or hearing about incest, rape, bondage. This is a common experience when one's first sexual acts were associated with exploitative violation. We are not in control of our thoughts and feelings, but we are in control of our behavior; there is no right or wrong when it comes to thoughts and feelings, but there can be a right or wrong when it comes to behavior. Therefore, I think it is important for survivors to rethink their sexual behavior if it includes violence, to determine whether the acts are replicating the abusive relationship or are simply erotic unto themselves.

Reclaiming one's sexual self is a scary but rewarding process. We live in a culture that has stripped us of our sexual selves, yet we as women are entitled to own our bodies. We have a right to reunite our heads with our bodies.

INTIMACY

As I have mentioned, intimacy and sex are often confused. Sex may be a way of expressing intimacy and connecting intimately with another human being, but it is not a requirement for intimacy. We can have sex with a stranger and not be intimate. We can be intimate with a family member and not be sexual. Sometimes they are connected but often they are not.

Intimacy implies honesty, vulnerability, trust, respect, connectedness, and openness. It is a particularly difficult area for survivors. When their earliest relationships were based on dishonesty, deceit, exploitation, and betrayal, it is not surprising that they have difficulty with intimacy as adults.

In addition to the scariness of intimacy, survivors sometimes do not have the social skills they need to begin the connection process. Very often incest survivors grew up in what we call "closed" family systems. A closed system is insular, with little outside information and few affiliations. One does not learn social connectedness when one is isolated from outside influences and interactions. Often survivors grew up in families in which outsiders were considered untrustworthy and dangerous, and so they had little opportunity to feel comfortable with strangers or acquaintances, and they may have had no opportunity to develop childhood friendships.

Even when survivors come from homes that modeled social graces and affability, the child often did not have an opportunity to practice these skills. She was to be seen and not heard, or she learned to be rebellious and bellicose as ways of keeping people away. Therefore in my work with survivors, sometimes we begin with acquiring basic social skills, which requires that the survivor be willing to begin taking small risks. The fact that a survivor has decided to seek therapy demonstrates to me that she has already begun to take risks. The fact that a survivor buys a book on incest recovery demonstrates her willingness to take some chances. Therefore, we begin to build on these initial successes in risk taking.

Betty, whom we met earlier in this chapter, came to therapy isolated and friendless. Her interaction with people was only in the context of her work. When not working, she was either alone or with her family of origin, with whom she had a difficult relationship. Her time alone was spent watching television. She described her apartment as in total disarray and gave that as one reason for not wanting to have friends, as they might stop over and see her chaotic home. After looking at the connection between chaos and her earlier sexual abuse (survivors are often experts on crisis and disorder and quite the novices on calm and harmony), Betty agreed that straightening up her house might be helpful. This eliminated one of her stated reasons for isolating herself.

After she organized her house, I suggested that she practice "shmoozing"—a beginning social skill that involves some risk and includes talking about relatively superficial subjects. We practiced some shmoozing techniques, such as commenting to someone, while in line at the supermarket, "These trash newspapers are hysterical. Look at this headline, 'Boy Scout Travels With Martian For Three Days'" or calling out to a neighbor, "Beautiful day today, don't you think?" This was a scary process for Betty, yet she knew that she needed to learn these skills before she could develop intimate relationships. She practiced shmoozing during the days between therapy sessions and reported back to me on her successes and deficiencies. She gained confidence with each success and additional information when the task seemed too difficult. Betty has graduated from shmoozing, to talking, to connecting with people. Over time, she developed several women friends with whom she now visits in her home and in theirs, and she has begun to participate in other activities that also put her in the company of others. Although she occasionally retreats from people, she continues to work on this area. Her television has been broken for several weeks, and she has not been particularly eager to fix it. She has recently joined an Adult Children of Alcoholics group and is beginning to experiment with "shmoozing" with men in the group. She does not feel ready to be intimate with a member of the opposite sex, but she does see that as a possibility in the future. Betty made great progress in this area because she was willing to take small risks, build on her successes, work on her self-esteem, and continue to take bigger risks. With each success, she learns to trust herself and gains confidence.

Practicing social skills, taking risks, and learning to be open require the survivor to learn to trust her instincts and to believe that she is a worthwhile person. Problems with intimacy are tied into feelings of self-worth. When one does not feel like a lovable, likeable, befriendable person, one does not trust others to be careful with her feelings or her person. How can someone trust another when she doesn't believe herself to be deserving of intimacy? Yet it is not surprising that survivors suffer from feelings of worthlessness and badness, when their earliest relationships created and reinforced negative beliefs about themselves. As children, besides learning that people can't be trusted, survivors learned that they had nothing worth giving to another but their bodies. They did not learn the lessons necessary for self-esteem—that they were strong, smart, wonderful, good, lovable. Attention and praise were conditional. Therefore it is necessary for survivors to be involved with self-esteem-building exercises. They need to learn that they were given faulty information as children. And they *were* given faulty information. They were not bad or unlovable; they were exploited by someone who was willing to hurt them in order to maintain the tyranny necessary to sexually abuse them.

Risk taking is an important part of intimacy. Sometimes survivors take incredible, dangerous risks, like "living life in the fast lane" as a way of punishing themselves or reinforcing their "bad girl" beliefs about themselves. This is *not* the risk taking to which I am referring. In fact, this type of risk taking, trusting the wrong people, is counter to intimacy and is quite common among survivors. I urge survivors to stop this type of risk taking immediately.

The risk taking I am suggesting begins with small steps and progresses: trusting someone to return a loaned book; trusting someone to do what she or he says they will do; trusting someone to listen to her when she needs an ear; trusting someone to come to dinner; trusting someone to get to know the survivor better; trusting others enough to get to know them better; trusting someone with her feelings; trusting someone to be honest. This is a progression that moves forward with each success. This is a process in which the survivor determines whether her intuitions are on target. It is a chance to listen to "uh-oh" feelings and to determine whether they are based on her present situation or on her past abusive situation. This is where a therapist may be helpful as a sounding board and a reality check.

Sometimes risk taking develops into testing others in ways that sabotage intimacy. Sometimes survivors have such an expectation of betrayal that they set up a series of tests for the people in their lives. As each test is passed, a more difficult task is presented, until finally the impossible is asked. This is often a subconscious process, and the survivor is not consciously aware of what she is doing. She may continue to test boundaries until the other person has no other choice but to disappoint her.

Sometimes the survivor sets up a no-win situation in which it is impossible to prove oneself trustworthy. An example of this might be a client asking her therapist to come to a party. If the therapist comes to the party, the survivor may feel betrayed because the therapist didn't keep the boundaries. If the therapist doesn't come, the survivor might feel betrayed because her therapist didn't attend this important event and thus proved that she really didn't care about her client. The therapist has been placed in a no-win situation in which any action will prove the survivor's belief that people can't be trusted.

Issues of trust and intimacy often come up in the therapy session, so I make predictions about trust early on. Besides clearly stating my boundaries, I let my clients know in the beginning of our relationship that trust is often an issue for childhood sexual abuse survivors. As mentioned previously, they often trust the wrong people or don't trust the right people. When trust/mistrust issues come up in therapy, I say, "Look, here it [trust/mistrust] is, just as I predicted." (This will be discussed more fully in chapter 12.)

Trust is a necessary ingredient of intimacy. Yet mistrust is necessary for women's survival—women must learn to mistrust in order to protect themselves from exploitation, assault, and danger. This is a conflict, in that what may be life-affirming in one regard can be life-threatening in another. Therefore, I think a survivor must learn to listen to body cues that alert her to danger. It is necessary to develop intimate relationships slowly, beginning with low-risk interactions and taking more chances only when she feels comfortable. It is important to understand the concept of safety first and to learn that safety and intimacy are not mutually exclusive.

The desire to be intimate is basic to humans, yet it is very frightening because we have to be willing to be hurt at times. It is impossible not to get hurt in an intimate relationship. This does not mean, however, that one has to be harmed. It does mean that intimacy brings up feelings. Some feelings are pleasant—love, joy, trust, concern. Other feelings are unpleasant—anger, hurt, sadness, disappointment. But in spite of the risks of disturbing feelings, intimacy is a vehicle for becoming connected to others in a way that enhances our lives. It is the necessary ingredient for a full and rewarding life. And although intimacy has been stolen from survivors by their abusive perpetrators, it is well worth the time, effort, and risk it takes to retrieve it.

CHAPTER ELEVEN

Special Lesbian Issues

For the most part, incest recovery is the same process for heterosexual women and for lesbians. Issues of trust versus mistrust, sex, intimacy, flashbacks, memory, intense feelings, as well as specific recovery steps, are the same. However, there are several matters that are special to survivors who are lesbians, and although for the most part sexual orientation in itself is not a factor in the incest recovery process, these matters need to be addressed.

Incest survivors often feel different from the rest of the world. They feel as if they do not belong and often attempt to be perfect and so "normal" that attention will not be drawn to them. In our heterosexist culture, lesbians, too, feel different. This impacts greatly on the identity of the lesbian who is also an incest survivor. Her knowledge of herself as a survivor of incest and her knowledge of herself as a lesbian reinforce her feelings of being different. What may result is an incest survivor attempting to deny her lesbian identity in order to fit in.

Robin, twenty-three, spent years denying her lesbianism by being sexual with numerous men. "My goal was that it [incest] wouldn't affect my life—certainly not my relationships. I was gonna be normal—perfect, too. I often wonder how that played on being a lesbian earlier or even thinking about it. I find it interesting. I never thought about the possibility earlier, because that would have meant to me that the incest was why I was a lesbian."

Robin demonstrates that a lesbian may deny her sexual orientation not only so as not to appear different but also because she may be afraid that the childhood sexual abuse she suffered caused her sexual orientation. This fear is a result both of living in a homophobic culture and of one's internalized homophobia, which of course are interwoven. To believe that incest *causes* lesbianism is to imply that lesbianism is an affliction rather than a healthy, comfortable option for women. Since lesbians live in a culture that promotes negative stereotypes of and encourages discrimination against lesbians and gay men, is it any wonder that they may suffer from internalized homophobia? Self-hatred by members of oppressed minorities is not uncommon. Many lesbians are actively working on overcoming their internalized homophobia. When one is also an incest survivor, this process is compounded—the lesbian survivor must work on two fronts, being both a lesbian and an incest survivor, in a misogynist, homophobic world.

In fact, sexual orientation does not seem to be influenced by childhood sexual abuse. Diana Russell's research (1982), conducted with 930 women in the general population, found 38 percent of the women interviewed to be survivors of childhood sexual abuse. Joann Loulan's research (1987) conducted with 1,566 lesbians found that 38 percent of the women identified themselves as having been sexually victimized as children. The identical percentages confirm the view that childhood sexual abuse has no bearing on adult sexual orientation.

Yet in spite of the fact that their view is not supported by any research, some lesbians believe that their sexual orientation is the result of childhood sexual abuse. Some believe that had they not been sexually abused by a man they would have a "healthy" relationship to men and that it is their fear of men that causes their sexual orientation. Others believe that had they not been sexually abused by a woman they would have related sexually to men and that they are lesbians because their first sexual experience was with a woman. In neither case does research confirm the connection they draw between sexual victimization and sexual orientation. The connection is based on the misconceptions of a culture in which heterosexuality is assumed to be the healthy norm, and in which lesbian existence is assumed to be an unhealthy deviance in need of explanation. This disservice has profound implications for everyone, not least for the lesbian engaged in the incest recovery process.

Sexual orientation is an important part of us. To deny our sexual orientation is to deny who we are. Therefore it is important to examine one's sexual orientation as part of the incest recovery process. For heterosexual women this is not a particular issue, as we live in a world of assumed heterosexuality. Heterosexual women do not usually have to identify sexual orientation as an issue, although some have questioned their sexual orientation during the recovery process. Lesbians, on the other hand, need to examine their sexual orientation and the internalized homophobia they may be experiencing. How can one recover from childhood sexual abuse without total self-acceptance? It is imperative that issues of homophobia, internalized homophobia, denial of sexual orientation, and acceptance of sexual orientation be addressed in order to help rebuild tattered self-esteem. Lesbian incest survivors need to embrace their sexual orientation as part of the recovery process.

Individual issues are not the only areas of difference between heterosexual incest survivors and lesbian incest survivors. There are some differences in relationship issues, too. For one thing, because of the prevalence of childhood sexual abuse among women, it is more likely that two incest survivors will couple in a lesbian relationship than in a heterosexual relationship. When they do, relationship problems may be intensified. In addition, even when only one member of the couple is an incest survivor, some relationship problems may be intensified because the survivor is a member of a same-sex couple.

Let's look first at the lesbian couple that has only one known incest survivor. (I use the word *known* because sexual abuse memory is often blocked.) If the survivor is filled with internalized homophobia as a result of her need to appear "normal," there may be a conflict within the couple about "coming out." This conflict can arise for any lesbian couple, whether childhood sexual abuse is an issue or not, and may be major; but when the couple includes a survivor, and the partner is "out" to her family, friends, and co-workers, the survivor, fearing a loss of normalcy with the coming-out experience, may be angry, threatened, or upset by her partner's openness. Whether to come out or not is often a delicate area for lesbians. When coming out feels like a threat to one's emotional well-being as an incest survivor, the conflict may be intensified. Yet if the partner knows the survivor's history and her feelings about being different and wanting to fit in, she may better understand the process of recovery and help to facilitate the survivor's self-acceptance as both a lesbian and an incest survivor.

Another area of conflict may be sex. Although many of the difficulties survivors have around sex are the same for heterosexual and lesbian couples, there may be additional difficulties for some lesbian couples. Sometimes lesbian survivors have the hope or belief that they will not have difficulties with sex because their childhood sexual abuse perpetrator was a man. This is usually not the case. Lesbians can also have flashbacks, surges of emotions, panic attacks, negative reactions to certain forms of touch even though they are engaged in sexual activities with women. These difficulties are the same as those experienced by heterosexual women, but they may feel even more overwhelming to the lesbian survivor who did not anticipate them. The survivor may feel betrayed by her sexual orientation and by her partner because she was not spared the trauma associated with sex. Without an understanding that reclaiming her body is part of incest recovery and that being sexual with a woman may not free her from flashbacks, anxiety, and other sexual issues, the lesbian survivor may become depressed and withdrawn. Her sexual difficulties may be compounded because she has the failed expectation that sex with a woman would not stir up the hurt and trauma from her childhood.

When two incest survivors couple, additional issues emerge. The issues that one incest survivor brings to a relationship are multiplied by two. This, combined with the excess baggage that any individual brings to any relationship, may make the relationship even more taxed than the relationship of a couple with only one survivor. As mentioned earlier, incest survivors often have issues around trust, sex and intimacy, depression, anger, and other intense feelings. When both members of the couple are survivors, these areas may clash. For instance, if the partners are in different stages of recovery (which often is the case), they may not be patient or understanding of one another's process. If they are in similar emotional places—for example, if they are both in the anger stage—their relationship may feel too intense.

When two survivors couple and bring to the relationship related sexual abuse issues, some patterns may emerge. For instance, it is not uncommon for survivors to have problems trusting—especially trusting people who love them. Sometimes survivors set up tests for people in anticipation of the betrayal they believe is coming. When both members of the couple are engaged in this activity, they may find themselves spending a lot of energy and time testing and being tested. They may take turns sabotaging the relationship, since each of them anticipates that she will be abandoned in the end. If this goes unidentified and unchecked, the relationship will become strained.

Since childhood sexual abuse issues impact on other aspects of the relationship between lesbian survivors, it is not surprising that the sexual arena is also affected. As mentioned previously, lesbian survivors are sometimes surprised to find out that sex is problematic even though they are being sexual with a woman. When both partners are survivors, they may both feel betrayed by this discovery.

When both partners are incest survivors, they may have difficulties with sex at different times. When one feels a need to be celibate, the other may not. When the survivor who previously needed celibacy is ready to be sexual again, her partner may desire to abstain from sex. The result may be a couple that is asexual for a long time. This may put additional stress on the couple and make long-term commitment difficult to maintain. Women in general often have issues around sex and may feel inhibited or distressed by sex, so a lesbian couple who becomes asexual for a prolonged period may not be responding to childhood sexual abuse. But certainly survivors who couple run a greater risk of having periods when sex is identified as a problem in their relationship.

This is not to say that lesbian relationships cannot thrive when one or both of the partners are survivors, but rather that there may be pitfalls that need to be addressed and overcome. Recognition of potential problems is the first step in safeguarding an important relationship. Understanding and acknowledging the issues can help keep the relationship on course. Seeking assistance through individual therapy and couple therapy may help the relationship survive the sexual abuse recovery process.

There is one more area that may impact on the individual lesbian sexual abuse survivor as well as the lesbian couple—support. Our homophobic society makes affirmation for lesbians very difficult; lesbians, particularly lesbian couples, do not get the support of the culture. This lack of support may replicate the lack of family support that the survivor felt as a child. Additionally, the mainstream culture's defamations of lesbians and gay men may replicate the abusiveness of the survivor's family of origin. In addition to the lack of cultural support, sometimes there is no family support for lesbians. For a survivor, this, too, may stir up the feelings of rejection and abandonment that were born in her childhood. These feelings may in turn complicate her sexual abuse recovery. Of course, if a survivor decides to distance herself from her family in order to continue to heal from childhood sexual abuse, the issue of her family's lack of support regarding her sexual orientation may be moot.

Although certain issues are compounded for lesbian survivors, being a lesbian does not necessarily hinder the sexual abuse recovery process. In fact, for many survivors their lesbian identity has facilitated their recovery. Denying her sexual orientation is detrimental for the lesbian sexual abuse survivor, but embracing it is, as for all lesbians, an empowering experience. Self-acceptance is critical for survivors, and the lesbian survivor who claims her sexual orientation has taken an important step on behalf of her own recovery.

Robin, whom we met earlier in the chapter, discussed the steps in her recovery process. "Claiming my lesbian identity I've found to be incredibly helpful, and I'm not sure why. It's been very empowering in lots of ways. I think I've felt more honest with myself. Being more honest with myself, I can be more open and honest with others."

Additionally, once the lesbian survivor embraces her sexual orientation and stakes a claim to her lesbian identity, she begins to reevaluate more of the culture's messages and assessments. She learns how poisonous homophobia is and how prejudice and hatred of all kinds breed injustice and evil. This reevaluation helps her to reassess her opinions and beliefs and to understand the connection between power and abuse. She may be better able to link the cause of her childhood victimization to the abuse of power by her perpetrator as she continues to make these connections within her adult world.

Self-acceptance does not happen automatically. To counteract the negative messages of our culture, lesbians need to look for positive role models. Internalized homophobia can be counteracted by reading lesbian literature, including biographies, essays, fiction, poetry, and periodicals, participating in lesbian political and social events, networking with other lesbians, and working with a therapist who accepts lesbianism as a positive option for women.

Coming out as a lesbian is an ongoing process. Every time one meets a new person, the decision to come out or not is considered. Although whether or not to come out is an individual decision and not a matter of right or wrong, I believe that lesbians in general and lesbian survivors in particular benefit by being out in at least some aspects of their lives. To be closeted implies that being a lesbian is something to be ashamed of, just as some survivors are ashamed of having been victims of sexual abuse. Claiming one's identity as a lesbian, no less than claiming one's identity as a survivor, counteracts the shame that is inherited from our patriarchal culture.

As I have said, being a lesbian does not in itself mean one's recovery will be hampered. In fact, when a lesbian has embraced her sexual orientation, she may find it easier to get support from and give support to women. And the ability to network with women and to see women as our source of strength is an essential ingredient in the incest recovery process.

CHAPTER TWELVE

Therapists: Working with the Survivor

There seem to be three distinct ways in which the psychological community has viewed incest. The earliest viewed reports of childhood sexual abuse as the fantasies of malicious, vengeful little girls who made false accusations against innocent men. When the psychological community began to recognize that childhood sexual abuse was a reality, a "pathological perpetrator" was named as the cause—sexual abuse was said to be committed by a few "crazy" men. When the psychological field discovered that childhood sexual abuse, particularly incest, was occurring in "good" homes as well as in the homes of society's "outcasts," a "dysfunctional family" was blamed, and incest was portrayed as the result of a family gone wrong, with the implication that each member of the family, including the abused child, had a piece of the incestuous problem. This is what Louise Armstrong (1982) termed "no-fault abuse." It may be more appropriate to call it "everybody's-fault" abuse. There are people, even today, who believe one or another of these views.

Because of the feminist movement, there are those of us who have moved beyond blaming the victim, beyond denying the problem, and beyond blaming the family system, to naming the violence. This has freed childhood sexual abuse survivors to set out on a path of recovery that leads them to the understanding that they were powerless within their families and that they can heal with or without their families' permission or approval. In naming the violence—that sexual abuse is the by-product of a patriarchal society—women are working toward a safer future for themselves and others. Psychotherapists can play an important role in this process.

This chapter explores general and specific ways the therapist can facilitate the survivor's recovery process. One of the most important things a therapist can do is believe the survivor when she says she was sexually abused. Most survivors report that as children they didn't tell anyone because they didn't think they would be believed. The ones who did tell often report that they weren't believed. Even as adults, many survivors find that other people have difficulty believing the atrocities that occurred in their childhood.

Before the therapist can believe the survivor, the therapist must know that something happened. This knowledge may not arise on its own, because some survivors have no memory of the abuse, and some who do have memory of it do not disclose their sexual abuse history. Sexual abuse recovery must begin with intake. As part of history taking, *every* client needs to be asked about her childhood sexual abuse history. This should be done in a nonpejorative manner with such questions as, How old were you when you had your first sexual experience? When you were a child, did you ever have sex with an adult? Do you recall being touched as a child in a way that made you feel uncomfortable? Even these nonjudgmental questions may not elicit responses about childhood sexual abuse. It may be more appropriate to ask about general household customs and rituals as a way of gently prodding the client's memory.

For therapists to be helpful to their survivor clients, they need to familiarize themselves with the experience of being sexually abused as a child. Incest and childhood sexual abuse survivor literature can be very helpful in this area. Therapists need to learn the symptoms and effects of childhood sexual abuse. They need to honor their clients' survival skills and understand that the "symptoms" of the survivor are normal responses to abnormal childhoods. They need to help their clients understand the results of the trauma and the nature of the recovery process.

Symptoms of childhood sexual abuse are depression, chronic depression, impulsivity, and dissociation. Survivors of chronic abuse may suffer from multiple personality, borderline personality, or masochistic personality. Effects of the incest may include alcohol and drug abuse, a history of revictimization, self-inflicted injury, suicide attempts, flashbacks, high anxiety, vomiting, stomach pains, anorexia nervosa, bulimia, or compulsive overeating. Survivors may be overly responsible, with a need to be perfect, or they may be totally helpless; they may be highly sexual or totally asexual; they may be distrustful of everyone or trustful of everyone without being able to make distinctions; they may be isolated, or they may be constantly in the company of others. They may swing back and forth between these polar opposites. This list of symptoms and effects is not to be seen as a list of pathologies but rather as a list of ways survivors have devised to endure their childhoods.

Although survivors may bring to therapy patterns of behaviors and thoughts that may be dysfunctional, they also bring many strengths. They are generally insightful, determined, caring, resourceful, creative people. Additionally, many survivors do not have any of these symptoms listed above, which is why I recommend that *all* clients be asked about their sexual abuse history. If we, as therapists, do not get this information early on, we may never get it, because many survivors try to "protect" themselves and their therapists from their own histories.

Before examining treatment issues and the specifics of individual, couple, and group therapy, the issue of trauma needs to be discussed. Often sexual abuse survivors suffer from post traumatic stress disorder. PTSD, a diagnosis that is commonly associated with war victims, results when, at the moment of trauma, time stopped. The trauma is re-experienced as recurrent, intrusive replays of the event. It is not surprising that childhood sexual abuse survivors would suffer from PTSD, since they have been the casualties of a war they weren't fighting, a war waged by adults against innocent children. Symptoms of PTSD are irritability, startle reactions, flashbacks, dream disturbances including nightmares, withdrawal and emotional numbness, and explosive aggressive behavior or helpless rage. Generally, when men suffer from PTSD they act out, whereas women who suffer from PTSD internalize the trauma and often become severely depressed, self-destructive, and withdrawn.

When a child suffers chronic trauma, she is likely to have some or all of the symptoms described above. She was a victim in a state of captivity under her perpetrator. It was as if she were held hostage in the family. There is a whole psychology of being held hostage that explains the symptoms of this chronic trauma. Yet psychology has been slow to understand the effects on children who are held captive by powerful adults—the perpetrators. Sexual abuse survivors are the returned hostages who never got the welcome and understanding that they deserved. It is this chronic abuse that has a lasting effect on the survivor. The survivor *is* scarred for life, but the recovery process will help to eliminate permanent damage.

Survivors of childhood sexual abuse were victimized as children. As therapists, we need to help them understand that they were not responsible for their victimization, regardless of whether they felt sexual pleasure or pain and of whether they were kept in enforced captivity or "decided" to continue to see their perpetrators. We can help our clients understand this by looking at the means of control that was used to maintain them in a condition of chronic trauma.

In childhood sexual abuse, methods of control include violence, threats of violence, enforced dependency, intermittent rewards, attention, involvement in the subjugation of others, the destruction of the mother–daughter bond, and isolation. These result, over time, in the child being immobilized by fear.

Amy's description of her uncle's abusiveness illustrates this point. "I was asked to take dinner down to him, and he would stick tinker toys in my private areas. Once he had my hands tied to the bedposts. I have an image of a knife swinging. He was in the corner masturbating." She is beginning to understand why she would "voluntarily" go down into her family's basement room where her uncle lived. "I felt completely left out in my family. I had one connection—my uncle. Sometimes he was real nice. Other times he was real sick. It was almost worth the gamble." Her uncle's means of control were violence, intermittent reinforcement, and taking advantage of the cold divisions within her family of origin. It's important that we as therapists understand this and help our clients to discover how tyranny was maintained by the perpetrator.

INDIVIDUAL THERAPY

As mentioned previously, incest recovery therapy begins with intake by getting a complete history. In constructing a genogram (family tree), I ascertain the family's history of domestic violence, substance abuse, psychiatric hospitalizations, medication, noteworthy family events, *and* a sexual abuse history.

If the client is a childhood sexual abuse survivor, I note what she brings to therapy, and I identify that for her as well. For instance, survivors generally have not learned to trust appropriately. They often trust the wrong people, if they trust anyone at all, and do not trust the right people. A survivor is someone who was both abused and neglected. I am aware that she may be asking herself about me, "Which will you be—the abuser or the neglecter?" I identify this question for her. I point out that she was not properly cared for as a child and has probably not learned to trust appropriately. She has learned, "People who love me, hurt me." I let her know that I expect that trust will be an issue we will have to work on and that there will be times when she may test me. Later in therapy if mistrust comes up, I can point it out and let her know that here it is, just as predicted.

Besides identifying trust issues for the client, I am also aware that I need to safeguard any trust gained throughout our work together. I take this responsibility seriously and do not promise what I can't deliver. One survivor came to me after a failed therapeutic relationship with a young inexperienced counselor. The counselor had told the survivor that she would *always* be there for her. Needless to say, no one can always be there for anyone, and the survivor quickly proved that to be the case. After she *proved* that the counselor couldn't be trusted, she came to me for therapy. Besides talking to her about trust issues, I made it a point to tell her that I could be her cheerleader but she was the one who needed to do the work. I *could not* always be there for her. Although I was tested in other areas, she didn't attempt to prove that I would not be there for her. We continued our work together in relative harmony.

Another issue I bring up with clients is the issue of boundaries. Because boundaries were nonexistent for the survivor as a child, she may not be able to distinguish between what is appropriate and what is not appropriate. She may have particular trouble knowing and keeping her own boundaries. The therapist must be her role model for boundary setting. She or he must have clear boundaries and keep them. Therapists should not have dinner with their clients, attend parties with their clients, play racquetball with their clients. Survivors have had their boundaries violated, and it is imperative that the therapist does not replicate that violation.

A third issue is that of intimacy. As I discussed earlier, survivors often mistake sex for closeness and vice versa. Therefore I make it a point to explicitly state to my clients early on in therapy that I will not harm them, hit them, or have sex with them. Additionally, I do not touch clients or hug clients unless I am asked to. Although this may seem rigid, I am aware that many survivors feel violated by touch, others get confused by touch, and still others have been exploited by other therapists via touch. I believe that warmth and caring can be demonstrated in other ways. And by not hugging a client unless asked, I can help the client to ask for what she needs rather than having her wait for others to figure out what she is wanting.

After intake and the identification of possible therapy issues, the recovery process continues. The therapist must move slowly and cautiously, allowing the survivor control at all times. Clients must be phys-ically and emotionally safe. The therapist must listen and allow the client to ventilate. The therapist must validate the story for her client and assure her that incest happens frequently, that it is traumatic, but that it can be dealt with. Childhood sexual abuse survivors do recover. Additionally I remind the survivor that although the recovery process is scary and painful, she has already survived the worst—the actual sex-ual abuse.

As mentioned previously, it is important for the therapist to help identify ways the abuse was maintained in the household. To do this the therapist must listen not only to the facts but also to the dynamics of the family system. She or he must identify for the client how the family's and other adults' behavior were tools to gain and keep con-trol over the child. She or he must focus not only on how violence and threats of violence maintained the terror but also on how atten-tion and rewards accomplished the same.

In conjunction with the above issue, it is also important that the therapist see the perpetrator and family members through the eyes of the survivor. (This is also true when working with children who have been sexually abused.) Initially the survivor may be angry at her mother, for not protecting her, and feel love and understanding for her perpetrator, particularly if he is her father. We do a disservice to our client if we push her prematurely toward the understanding that her mother was probably powerless in the family and unable to pro-tect her. Additionally, we fail our clients when we push them to rage at their perpetrators. To paraphrase Judith Herman (1986), if we, as therapists, express our anger at the perpetrator when the survivor feels love toward him, we make the survivor feel like a prostitute who feels guilty for loving her pimp.

We need to follow the survivor's pace and the survivor's cues during the recovery process. As individual therapy progresses and we continue to examine the dynamics of the family, the survivor will probably reassess her family of origin. This reassessment will result in her identifying her perpetrator's responsibility in the abuse and in a better understanding of her mother's power or lack of power within the family. For the survivor who feels guilty for her "complicity" in the abuse, this reassessment will help her understand that she, also, was powerless in the family. Regardless of how strongly she believes she could have prevented or stopped the abuse, the fact is she was a young child unable to control her perpetrator.

The goal of therapy is to help the survivor assume control over her life. Control and autonomy are essential for the survivor. This is facilitated in the process of therapy itself when the therapist recognizes the survivor as the expert on her condition. The survivor must be the one who determines the time and pace of her recovery process. She must work through the stages of recovery at her own pace.

The therapist must also help the client recognize her survival skills, to understand that what she and others may have seen as pathological were the necessary tools she used to help her make it through her childhood. During this process the client needs to examine these survival skills to determine which of them she may still need and which she no longer needs. For instance, as mentioned earlier, cutting oneself in order to localize the pain may no longer be a helpful coping method, but being attentive to details in the environment may be essential for her continued well-being.

Besides identifying survival skills, it is necessary for the survivor to recognize the rules she has created because she grew up in a family in which she was not protected from abuse. For instance, "People who love me, hurt me" is a global rule, a belief one might accept as a universal truth, learned in childhood. By identifying and analyzing these rules, the survivor can determine how they may be keeping her from a fulfilling life. If one has internalized the above rule, for example, it would be difficult to establish and maintain satisfying relationships.

Sandy, age forty-six, entered into therapy because of her incest history. In addition her marriage was troubled. She and her husband communicated very little, had no sex, and rarely had fun together. Sandy was isolated and depressed. One day she came into our session and explained that she was upset because someone at work had put several cartoons about therapy and rocky marriages into her mailbox. She was hurt because she felt that whoever gave her the cartoons was making fun of her painful situation. I then asked her to finish this sentence, *People are . . .* , and she said, "People are basically evil and out to get me." She had identified her global rule—and like most of us, she viewed the world in a way that would prove her global rule to be true. I pointed out that someone who had the global rule "People are usually good and are trying to do right by me" may have viewed those cartoons as a way of trying to help make a difficult situation lighter through humor. I emphasized that only the person who put the cartoons in her mailbox knew the motivation behind that gesture. The next week, Sandy came into session and explained that her co-worker who put the cartoons in her mailbox heard that she was upset and apologized. The co-worker said she had been trying to cheer Sandy up, and further explained how difficult it was for her to choose a birthday card for Sandy because she was so afraid that she would hurt Sandy's feelings. For Sandy, this interaction clarified how her global view, "People are out to get me," had kept people at bay. Of course, it was understandable, based on her childhood violation, why it felt safer to keep people at bay. But Sandy recognized that she wanted to have meaningful and intimate relationships and needed to learn to distinguish between trustworthy and untrustworthy people. She began to examine how her global rule had served her and how it may not always serve her in all interactions.

Survivors may also have questions that they do not articulate. It is important for the therapist to make these questions known if they are not identified specifically by the client. There are three common questions that survivors have and need to answer to help the recovery process proceed: Was I responsible? Why didn't I make it stop? Am I damaged for life? The answers are: No; Because you were powerless; and No. But first, before the answers will come, the questions need to be established.

The therapist's job is to listen, to bear witness, and to predict what may occur during the recovery process. The therapist needs to point out that survivors sometimes regress to old behaviors and feelings. This warning is extremely helpful; it will enable the survivor to be less alarmed and more understanding if and when old behaviors resurface, and it may prevent the resurfacing of coping skills that are no longer helpful for the recovery process.

I had a client who was a recovering alcoholic. She had had seven years of sobriety when she entered into incest recovery therapy. Throughout our initial work together, I pointed out how survivors often regress to old behaviors during incest recovery and suggested that she return to her AA meetings. She insisted that her sobriety was very secure and she no longer needed meetings. In spite of my warnings and her years of sobriety, she had a slip and found it necessary to enter a residential alcohol treatment program. We continued our incest recovery work after her completion of alcohol treatment, however, and she now is involved in regular AA meetings and has identified a sponsor.

It is important that the therapist be a calm listener who can bear witness, validate the survivor's experiences and emotions, and assure the survivor that what she is experiencing is normal and will pass.

The survivor needs to bear affect, bear the memory of the abuse, make new meaning out of her abusive childhood, and renegotiate her place in her family of origin. She will succeed at this as she continues to work with an empathetic, caring professional who allows her the control and positive regard she deserves.

Therapists can introduce specific ways of facilitating the recovery process, including relaxation techniques, ego-building exercises, guided imagery, and bibliotherapy. Some examples of relaxation techniques are specific relaxation tapes, deep-breathing exercises, and calming, hypnotic exercises. Ego-building exercises include specific tasks that focus on the survivor's strengths, positive feedback, and specific assignments that guarantee success. Guided imagery produces specific calming fantasies that can help the survivor create peaceful spaces within her life. Bibliotherapy uses specific literature that addresses therapeutic issues, such as survivor literature, recovery literature, and self-help books.

It will also be beneficial for the therapist to help the survivor remember a positive, nurturing person, particularly a woman, who was involved in her childhood. It's important to identify a woman for two reasons. First, survivors healing from sexual abuse benefit from networking with other strong women; their identities are strengthened through their connections to women. Second, this woman-figure, if internalized by the survivor, can become a role model who will help her learn to properly parent herself. If an adult or older child cannot be identified, a favorite pet or doll can substitute as a means of locating someone or something that could give and receive love when everything else was cold and uncaring.

During individual therapy, the survivor can work on specific issues. In the beginning stages, the focus is on the survivor telling her story. The heart of our work together revolves around trust building, ego building, validating the survivor's experiences, storytelling, and strengthening the survivor's internal and external resources. During the initial stages, she may experience a period of intense grief and sadness. She may become suicidal or decide to stop therapy because the intensity feels too overwhelming. If she becomes actively suicidal, hospitalization may be necessary. During this grieving process, the survivor may begin to reevaluate the members of her family and may be overcome with deep emotions.

It is during this beginning stage that I am prepared to be available by phone twenty-four hours a day. (I am available throughout therapy, but emergency phone calls diminish as the recovery process proceeds.) When the survivor emerges from this stage—and she will emerge—she is stronger and more capable of continuing the difficult recovery work that is ahead for her.

During the middle stage of therapy, I become more directive. After empathetic listening, validation of the survivor's experiences and emotions, and helping her to identify her strengths, I begin to focus on ways to facilitate the healing of her wounds from her childhood devastation. We work on specific ways of reclaiming her body by means of a focused plan of action. We work on her relationships, including those with family and friends. We focus on specific activities that facilitate movement through the different emotional states—depression, anger, sadness, letting go, and so on. And we work on specific tasks and exercises described in previous chapters.

During this stage, if it hasn't happened earlier, specific details of the sexual abuse are discussed. It is important that this occur in order for the survivor to normalize her current state and explode the secret that she has been carrying, and as a way to help her put the abuse in perspective. Also, as she discusses the specifics of the childhood trauma, she may reclaim additional memories that will expedite the recovery process.

During this middle stage the issue of confrontation comes up. If she has never confronted her perpetrator or family, she may now begin to ponder confrontation as an option. Confrontation is not for everyone, and it is not necessary for recovery, but it can be an empowering experience for the survivor. If the survivor chooses to confront, however, the confrontation needs to be carefully planned. The client must be prepared for anything. Most survivors hope that when confronted, the perpetrator will admit his wrongdoing and apologize for his abusive behavior and that the family members will believe her and support her in her recovery process. However, that scenario is unlikely. Often the perpetrator denies the abuse or claims that the survivor was a willing party to the sexual relationship. Sometimes family members reject the survivor and side with the perpetrator. The survivor needs to be prepared for this and to recognize that the success of a confrontation does not depend on the perpetrator's response or her family's response, but rather on the fact that by stepping forward she has changed her role with regard to them. Whatever her family does, the survivor is no longer acting in cooperation with her old family role of secrecy and responsibility. She has broken the family pattern of silence and denial.

Individual therapy can help the survivor work through the recovery stages, but group therapy is also important and can give survivors some things that can't be obtained through individual therapy. Sometimes individual therapy helps get the survivor ready for an incest recovery group. I believe it is important that when a client joins a survivors' group she continue her individual therapy as well. The possibility of entering group therapy should be discussed before the final stages of her individual therapy (see the discussion of group therapy later in this chapter).

Termination of therapy is an important part of the incest recovery process. Therapists must be aware that good-byes can be interpreted as abandonment. Ideally therapy is ended only when the client determines that she is ready to leave. Unfortunately, sometimes, because of bureaucratic constraints imposed by insurance companies and mental health agencies, therapy is available for only specific periods of time. I suggest when possible that therapy end gradually with weekly sessions becoming biweekly sessions, then monthly check-ins, and then termination. During the period of termination the therapist needs to articulate that endings sometimes feel like abandonment and that this is not abandonment but rather a new stage in the survivor's life. This period is the time to highlight what the client has accomplished during therapy and to evaluate her individual work. I explicitly express that I am available to her in the future. I let her know that during life stages, the trauma may be rearoused. If that occurs, therapy can always begin again.

The therapist's own attitudes are very important in the therapy process. I believe my success as a therapist working with survivors is enhanced by my ability to form warm, positive relationships with my clients. I sincerely believe that recovery is possible, and I emphasize my faith in survivors and the recovery process. Although the sexual abuse was traumatic and hurtful, I do not see working with survivors as depressing but rather as a privilege, in that I am working with strong, motivated women. I believe that my admiration and respect for my clients are evident.

Because I see this work not as depressing but rather as empowering, there are many times that I use humor in therapy. Further, my commitment to my work underlies my willingness to be available by phone to my clients on a twenty-four-hour basis.

GROUP THERAPY

Group therapy is the modality of choice for incest and childhood sexual abuse recovery. I strongly suggest, however, that group therapy occur in conjunction with individual therapy, because group sessions shared with eight women do not allow for all individual issues to be addressed. Group therapy can help the survivor address the issues of isolation, feeling different from the rest of the world, disclosure, forming networks, recovering memory, and telling others what she can't tell herself ("It wasn't your fault") in ways which cannot happen in individual therapy.

As mentioned earlier, incest survivors often are isolated and feel different from the rest of the world. They often believe that they are the only ones who have experienced childhood sexual abuse. They often think that they were sexually abused because they were bad and deserved to be abused. Barbara, who has been involved in ongoing recovery therapy, explains how these earlier feelings are sometimes still with her. "I still believe that people who grew up in good families deserved them. And because I was beaten and raped, that I deserved that. And it's very hard for me to emotionally separate those kinds of feelings from what is real, which is that my father was a fucking maniac."

Involvement in a survivor group helps the client to understand that she is not alone or different from other women. When she meets other survivors, she begins to recognize that the goodness or badness of the child does not determine the treatment she received from her family or the quality of her childhood. She learns that many women have experienced the same childhood trauma as she. Additionally, involvement in the group dispels the myth that incest survivors are "abnormal." Many survivors express to me their fear of finding themselves in a group with someone they know, as if they have something to be ashamed of or to hide. It is usually these clients who, in the first session, express to the group, "My God, you all are so normal." To connect with other strong women who are working on recovery is a wonderful normalizing process.

The connection to other survivors via a group also helps the survivor form networks. These networks will be extremely helpful as she struggles with different stages of recovery. Margaret, forty, explained an essential ingredient in her incest recovery process: "Helping other survivors heal. Having close friends who are also survivors who can cry with me and laugh with me." Involvement with other survivors is a wonderfully empowering, moving experience.

Working on incest recovery through survivor groups may also help some clients recover memory. Hearing other women's stories may stimulate new memories and restimulate old feelings. This process may be the catalyst for movement to another level of memory.

Another important aspect of group work is that survivors can tell others what they need to tell themselves. It is not uncommon for a woman to blame herself, in the course of a session, for complicity because when she was four she wore a miniskirt around her perpetrator, and at another session, say to another survivor, "How can you blame yourself? You were only six." When the group members can point out her inconsistency about guilt and responsibility, she may begin to recognize that she, too, was guiltless in the sexual abuse.

This necessary step in incest recovery may not happen without the group experience. Although a therapist who listens and points out family dynamics can help in the elimination of guilt, such help may not be as effective as hearing other survivors speak and hearing oneself say the words, "It was not your fault." Therefore, in spite of wonderful work that can be accomplished in individual therapy, survivor groups still remain the therapy of choice.

There are three types of groups that survivors have used in their recovery process: the self-help group, the social action group, and the therapist-led group.

SELF-HELP GROUPS

A self-help group is comprised only of survivors; leadership is either shared, alternated, or nonexistent. Generally there is no screening for the group, and everyone is welcome. The group is designed to allow childhood sexual abuse survivors the opportunity to talk about their abuse and to network with other survivors. Some self-help survivor groups are based on the Twelve Step concept (the Alcoholics Anonymous approach), others are not, and groups may be structured or open.

Although a self-help group may be a good alternative if a therapist-led group is unavailable, there are cautions that ought to be considered before joining. One concern that I have regards screening. Most self-help groups are open to anyone who chooses to come. It is my belief that not everyone is ready for a group experience. A woman who gets involved in a group prematurely may be retraumatized by the group experience. The other members, who are ready for a group experience, may not benefit from the group if someone who is not ready joins it. (See the criteria discussed in the section later in this chapter on therapist-led groups.) Additional problems may result if there is no objective person in the group to help facilitate the process, particularly when extremely painful emotions and experiences arise. Although I don't think there is any particular topic that should be avoided, sometimes survivors are too close to the issues and emotions that may arise to help facilitate someone else's process. These issues can be addressed by having a therapist or other objective person act as a consultant to the group, giving it support, supervision, and guidelines, and by having a different group member each week take on the role of facilitator, with specific guidelines for facilitating the group discussion.

SOCIAL ACTION GROUPS

A social action group, although not specifically therapeutic, can help in the recovery process. When survivors of sexual abuse network around a particular planned action, they may find the experience to be very empowering. Several years ago, a group of survivors in my area organized an incest speakout. The process of organizing and planning served as a vehicle for politicizing themselves around an issue of great importance and concern. Additionally it served as a "survivor's mission" in that the women were using their experiences as incest survivors to positively impact on their community.

THERAPIST-LED GROUPS

The focus of this section is the therapist-led, time-limited group. The therapist-led group is a highly structured group with a beginning, a middle, and an end. It is a safe environment for controlled regression, and it includes storytelling, intense feelings, giving and receiving empathy and validation, and the mobilization of internal and external resources.

When I am forming a group, I conduct intake interviews with all prospective members. The intake interview is a screening device that helps me assess the survivor's readiness for the group. I let her know that the interview is a chance for me to see if I can work with her and for her to see if she can work with me. I also let her know that the group experience is not for everyone and that our interview will help us to determine whether a survivors' group will be helpful to her at this time. I let her know that if she is not able to use the group now, the group will probably be helpful to her at a later point.

At the intake interview, I assess the survivor's strengths and weaknesses, and I screen out for psychosis, active drug abuse, and active alcohol abuse. I look to see whether the survivor can stay with me during the interview—that is, whether she can stay focused and coherent— and if she can discuss the incest. I am aware that premature treatment may be worse than no treatment at all, so I am careful to consider the appropriateness of the group experience for the particular woman. In my many years of facilitating incest survivor groups, I have screened out very few women. I have found that survivors who are considering a group usually know when they are ready to effectively utilize this kind of support.

When I begin a survivors' group, there are several things I consider. I am aware that childhood sexual abuse survivors often feel different from other people, so I make a strong attempt to have a mixed group and not, for example, a group of six heterosexual women and one lesbian, or seven white women and one African-American woman. I try to make sure there are at least two lesbians in a group or two minority women. Survivors have many issues around feeling like outsiders, as do lesbians and women of color because of our racist, homophobic culture, and the survivors' group should not reinforce anyone's feelings of being different.

I also carefully plan the number of participants. My survivors' groups consist of six to eight women plus myself as the facilitator. Two facilitators may be helpful because they can share leadership, perhaps give more individual attention, and act as role models of communication, boundaries, and conflict-resolution; but groups can also be led by a single therapist, and my groups are facilitated solely by me. Whether there is one facilitator or two, I believe that the optimum number for a survivors' group is not fewer than six and not more than eight members. Fewer than six runs the risk of being too small if there are absences, and more than eight may not allow for full participation by the members.

Once the screening is done and the members of the group are determined, the group begins. As I mentioned, I do time-limited groups. The group lasts for twelve weeks, with a thirteenth-week celebration. (The celebration idea comes from Sandra Butler, author of *Conspiracy of Silence*.) The number of weeks the group runs is somewhat arbitrary, and other therapists have groups that run for eight weeks, twelve weeks, sixteen weeks, or twenty weeks. But twelve weeks has worked best for me. I have found that survivors can commit themselves to three months of intense work. Fewer than twelve weeks doesn't give the group an opportunity to evolve into a cohesive unit, nor does it give the members a chance to work on specific goals and steps of recovery. More than twelve weeks sometimes seems overwhelming and too much of a long-term commitment to focus on the intensity of the childhood sexual abuse. Additionally, since I encourage members to be involved in individual therapy as well as group therapy, they can continue to work on the specific recovery stages after the group.

The group's work is divided into a beginning, a middle, and an end, and the group is highly structured, particularly in the beginning stage, to promote physical and emotional safety. The beginning sets the stage for intimacy and trust.

The therapist goes over ground rules in the first session. Ground rules are essential in that they set boundaries and are the framework for establishing safety. Here are some examples of ground rules: Confidentiality is required; do not come high to the group; participation in activities is voluntary; no violence in the group. Each therapist should determine what needs to be included in the ground rules. The content of the ground rules is less important than having the rules, since the purpose is to provide structure and guidance.

Also during the first session, each member identifies a small, tangible goal that she will work on during the weeks of the group. Some examples of tangible goals are the confrontation of the perpetrator, the disclosure of her incest history to a friend, telling her story to the group, or making a new friend. Goals that are intangible, such as being happy or letting go of anger, are not measurable and therefore do not help the survivor to focus on her successes. They can be fine-tuned however, so that they become more tangible. "Being happy," for example, can become "doing at least one activity a week that is solely for my pleasure"; instead of aiming to "let go of anger," a survivor can work on designing a ritual that will express her anger toward her perpetrator. Goals that are too lofty or unrealistic, such as writing a novel about incest or losing thirty pounds, are unreachable in such a short period and sabotage the success orientation of the group, but these, too, can be fine-tuned so that they are more realistic—for instance, the survivor can take on the task of creating an outline for a proposed book on incest or of not stuffing feelings down by eating refined sugar on group nights. The goals need to be success oriented, and therefore clients may need assistance in formulating them.

Additionally in the first session, the therapist identifies survivor symptomatology and explains that during the recovery process old emotions and behaviors may resurface. She or he should explain that at times symptoms and emotions may be severe, but that they are transient. In conjunction with this prediction, the therapist needs to explain the group process (how groups work) and the recovery process (expected stages of recovery) and identify questions the participants may have (Was I responsible? Why didn't I make it stop? Am I damaged for life?).

The first two sessions are structured to prevent catharsis. A first- or second-session catharsis may feel like a reenactment of the childhood trauma, and the survivor may feel too vulnerable and open. An early-session catharsis runs the risk of the survivor not returning to the group.

After the discussion of the ground rules and group process, a formal introduction of the group members is necessary. The more creative and fun this exercise can be, the better, as it will help relieve the tension that is very present in the room. Some therapists have suggested that clients introduce themselves through a favorite childhood story, others have suggested that clients introduce themselves by telling the group something that the group wouldn't know by just looking at them, and still others have suggested that members introduce themselves by identifying an accomplishment of the past month. The introduction is a way in which members can begin to know each other. An introduction exercise that includes childhood stories can get the members to begin focusing on childhood memories. An introduction exercise that includes accomplishments can help the survivor focus on her strengths.

In the beginning sessions (the first four sessions), raw data can be gathered through writing exercises and art work. This is a time for the survivor to begin to focus on her childhood in a controlled and safe manner. I introduce guided imagery and relaxation techniques to help the survivor gain the resources she will need in the later, more difficult work.

One thing I do as a way of building trust and helping the members gain inner resources is structure activities the survivor can do at her own pace and comfort level. For instance, I ask the survivor to do specific writing exercises to identify a strong woman figure from her childhood. If she does not have one, I ask her to create her—what would she be like if she existed. The strong woman figure, created or real, will help ease the pain during the emotional disclosure process. Each member tells the group of her strong woman figure. It's important for the survivor to have another person hear what she has written, and sharing stories may help other members remember details of their own childhoods that may have been lost for them. Through structured activities, the survivor can take steps toward building relationships by reading her writings, showing her art work, listening to others, and giving feedback and encouragement to group members.

In later sessions, through guided imagery and relaxation techniques, the survivor learns to create a safe place to which she can retreat when she needs a respite from the overwhelming emotions that may get stirred up. With this safe place, combined with her newfound inner resource (the strong woman figure) and her newfound outer resource (other sexual abuse survivors), she is ready to enter the middle stage of the group.

During the middle stage, feelings of guilt, anger, and grief may be very profound. These emotions emerge as the disclosure process begins. I structure a specific disclosure session in which the members of the group have quiet time to be alone with their thoughts and determine how they will disclose to the group.

There are different points of view about disclosure. Some therapists feel that specific disclosure may retraumatize the survivor and may be disrespectful to the survivor who does not have memory. My belief, however, is that specific disclosure is necessary. By speaking about the specifics of the sexual abuse, the survivor ends the burden of carrying a secret. Additionally, to avoid talking about the specifics seems to imply that the survivor has something to be ashamed of. By exploding the secret, we help to correct the notion that she needs to hide what happened from others. Finally, I believe that hearing the specifics of other survivors' abuse may help the survivor without memory to regain some, and she can disclose what she feels and has come to understand as the signs alerting her to her sexual abuse history.

The disclosure session is a time for the survivor to focus on her abuse and to design a way to confront it. The therapy room includes art material, paper, and musical instruments to allow the survivor varied ways to present her story. During the next few weeks, members take turns giving and receiving support and empathy as each woman discloses to the group.

During this time (the middle six weeks), the group is designed to give support for the expression of the profound emotions. Expression of support, telling others what one needs to tell herself, revving up internal and external resources, and open discussions help provide the necessary assistance during this painful yet empowering process. Rituals, psychodrama, structured exercises (particularly around specific emotions of guilt and anger) and anger-release activities, such as expressing outrage while beating a phone book with a piece of hose, are utilized to help the survivor work through the powerful emotions generated in these sessions.

During the latter part of this middle section, when trust and safety have been established and group members have formed caring, empathetic relationships, I am less prominent in the group. I may establish the framework for working through issues, but the individuals in the group creatively design ways of working through the issues. I remember one member of a group, Leslie, who designed an anger ritual. She created a circle and gave each member a percussion instrument. She explained to the group that she wanted to express her outrage at her uncle for having violated her. She asked that each member join her as they wished in releasing the anger and rage. She knelt in the middle of the circle pounding a pillow. As the group members spontaneously created a symphony of percussion sounds, they each called out support to Leslie and expressions of anger toward her perpetrator and toward their own perpetrators. This moving ritual could only take place because of the powerful connection among the women of the group.

I often structure activities in response to the issues that arise in these spontaneous, survivor-directed activities. I have used family sculptures, where a member creates a representation of her family by maneuvering and placing group members throughout the room and in relationship to each other; gestalt exercises, such as dialogues between different aspects of dreams; and psychodrama, where a group member might reenact a situation by using other group members to represent different people and places in her life. All of these can facilitate movement in the incest recovery process.

While working through grief, guilt, anger, and disclosure during this middle period, the survivor often renegotiates her role in the family. She reevaluates family members, and she considers whether or not to confront her perpetrator and disclose to her family. This is usually the time when the survivor takes powerful steps in her recovery process.

The ending of the group begins several weeks before the group actually ends. Survivors often interpret good-byes to be abandonment, and the therapist needs to point this out to the group, discuss the members' feelings about the group's ending, and remind them that they have established a network of support (the other group members) that can continue after the group has ended. I remind the group for several weeks that the end is coming. I state that there are three weeks left, then that there are two weeks left, and then that there is one week left. During the last two weeks, group members review what they have done, evaluate the group, restate and evaluate their goals (which was also done periodically throughout the sessions), and discuss the celebration that will occur after the group has ended. I leave open the option of getting involved in further therapy at a later point.

The celebration happens on the thirteenth week. This is an opportunity for the group members to honor what they have accomplished both as individuals and as a group. The celebration includes each member bringing some food to share and an intangible gift for the group. Some clients read poems they have written, others play instruments, still others share their different talents—all as a means of showing gratitude to the women who have supported them through this process. The celebration is an up time in which the members honor their scars, their process, and their accomplishments as sexual abuse survivors. Additionally, the celebration enables the process of saying good-bye to be a more positive experience.

There are some general points therapists must remember about running a survivors' group. First, the group must be highly structured. The therapist is very prominent in the beginning and early middle stages, and becomes less prominent only as safety and security are established.

Second, the group must be success oriented. Each session should end with an exercise focusing on the survivors' accomplishments. In the beginning stages of the group, the final task for the session may be for each member to identify something that has made her proud.

Later sessions may require the members to identify something they accomplished that week. In final sessions the survivors are asked to name something positive that happened to them that session. These later sessions help the survivors to give and receive positive feedback about their roles in each others' recovery process.

Third, the therapist must *move slowly*, listen, validate, be affirming, and allow for the expression of emotions. In particular, therapists should recognize that survivors often feel guilty. It is important for the therapist to point out that children are sexual beings and that feeling sexual pleasure does not mean complicity. The survivor needs to know that if the perpetrator wanted her to feel pleasure, she felt pleasure, and if he wanted her to feel pain, she felt pain. The therapist should help the survivor understand that she was powerless in the abusive relationship.

Additionally the therapist needs to validate and encourage the expression of anger. Women's anger is often trivialized within our culture, yet expressing anger can be very empowering. The survivor needs to know that women's anger is culturally ridiculed instead of encouraged. She needs to learn that she is entitled to her anger and that its expression can only be empowering. The survivor may need to learn how to appropriately express anger and may have to be given the tools to overcome her fears. One way of exploring her fears about anger is to examine how anger was expressed in her family of origin—who was allowed to get angry in her family of origin and who was not, how was the anger expressed, what was the response by family members to her childhood expression of anger, and so on. She should also examine her family of creation's response to anger—who's allowed to get angry now? [Although "family of procreation" is the accepted term in some schools of psychology to distinguish the family one creates from one's family of origin, I prefer "family of creation" to avoid the implication that the child-bearing function is the essence of families.]

The therapist may be heavily on-call during the initial weeks of the group. In time, as the survivors gain inner strength and create support networks, they will rely less on the therapist and more on their other resources.

As mentioned earlier, the use of a cofacilitator may be advantageous. Sharing the responsibility of the group can help prevent burnout and feelings of isolation, and can provide additional eyes to catch what's going on in the group. Together two therapists can role-model conflict-resolution and communication skills.

Facilitating survivors' groups has been a rewarding experience for me. It has given me the opportunity to work with strong, motivated women who make major changes in a relatively short period of time. And groups allow for wonderful, touching moments, intensely emotional sessions, and warm humor—they are powerful experiences in which women can cry and laugh together.

COUPLE AND FAMILY THERAPY

Since the incest survivor does not exist in a vacuum, her recovery process affects the significant people in her life—partners, children, mother, father, siblings, and friends. Sometimes the therapist and the survivor may decide to work with the supporting cast.

In my work with survivors in individual therapy, there are times when I also work with one or more members of the survivor's network. When we decide to bring in family members, I explicitly state at the beginning of the couple or family session that I am present for the survivor and that the others have been invited in to help us work more effectively. I state this immediately so as not to jeopardize my relationship with the survivor. Because survivors can easily feel abandoned—based on their childhood history of abandonment—I want to be sure my client does not interpret other people's participation in our session as an abandonment of her.

I see members of the survivor's network in order to help the survivor and to help me get information. The information obtained may be new, or may confirm what the survivor already knew. When a life partner is brought in, the session may focus on problematic areas in the relationship (sex, for example) and how the partner can help in the recovery process.

Sometimes family members may be invited to sessions for the purpose of confrontation or disclosure. If this is the goal, I ask another therapist to be present and to work with us. In this way, I can focus my attention and support on the survivor, and the other therapist can work with the family members and help them understand the reactions and feelings that are being generated by the session. These sessions are well planned; the survivor has prepared what she will say and do, and both therapists understand the roles they are to play. When such a session is planned, I make sure that I will be working with a therapist I know well and who has expertise in family therapy and group process.

If ongoing family therapy or couple therapy is in order, I refer the survivor and the other members to a couples therapist or family therapist. Sometimes the referral is to a (qualified, ethical) sex therapist. I continue to work with the survivor individually as she and her partner or family work with another therapist. However, it is advantageous to have the survivor sign a release form so that the therapists involved can consult and share information with one another when necessary.

It is important to note that incest survivors often become the "identified patient" in therapy. Since survivors so easily take the blame and responsibility when things go wrong, it is not uncommon for them to see themselves as the problem in their relationships. Unfortunately, family members and therapists sometimes fall into believing that false notion. Survivors have their problems and issues, and they bring them to relationships, but so do all members of families. It is important that the therapist prevent the survivor from maintaining the role of the identified patient. Recently when I saw a survivor and her husband for a session, the husband said he was very concerned about the amount of stress his wife had in her life. In a very sincere, concerned way he said he felt that if his wife were under less stress, their relationship would improve. I asked him if he were under any stress or strain, and he emphatically denied that there was any pressure at all in his life. As we continued talking I learned that he was a police officer in a major urban area, his father had just died, and he was in his second year of cancer remission. *But he was not feeling any stress.* Clearly the survivor was the identified patient in this couple, especially since she agreed that if she somehow changed, their relationship would be fine. Survivors and their families need to see that it is detrimental to the survivor and to the family to have her be seen as the problem.

COUNTERTRANSFERENCE

It's important to examine not only what the client brings to therapy, but also what the therapist brings. There often are some countertransference issues of which the therapist needs to be aware. Working with survivors of childhood sexual abuse can stimulate for the therapist basic feelings of terror, fear of abandonment, exploitation, and despair. Therapists are engaged in a process of bearing witness to tales of horror and devastation, and although it is true that survivors bring many strengths to therapy, they are involving the therapist in recording a history full of pain, confusion, and anguish. It's important that therapists realize that working with survivors can touch on issues that are close to them and that therapists need to take care of their feelings as well. Therefore, it is imperative that the therapist have a network of other healers who can give supervision and support to this important work.

Women therapists may sometimes be victim-identified—that is, be aware of their own vulnerability in this violent, patriarchal society. By reviewing the statistics, not to mention our own experiences, women know that they run the risk of physical and sexual assault, so it is not surprising that women therapists may have basic emotions of fear and terror restimulated when they are listening to survivors' stories of abuse. Sometimes this identification with the "victim" may produce profound anger toward the perpetrator. However, if the therapist vents her anger toward the perpetrator, she does not allow her client to express her ambivalence and love for him. The therapist's anger may make the survivor feel guilty for loving her abuser and could prevent her from exploring all of her feelings with the therapist.

Feminist therapists run the risk of discounting the survivor's rage toward her mother by seeing the mother as a victim. But raging at her mother for not protecting her is often a necessary step in the survivor's recovery process. If the therapist politicizes the mother as a victim (which she probably is), the client may protect the therapist from the client's feelings toward the mother. Therefore, the therapist needs to hold back. In time, as the client examines the dynamics of her family of origin, she will begin to reevaluate the roles of its members. At her own pace, she may see her mother as another powerless, frustrated casualty of this family. (Mothers are discussed in more detail in chapter 14).

Men therapists may identify with the perpetrator. They may find it difficult to hear the client's anger at her perpetrator, and they may be more comfortable hearing clients express anger toward themselves and their mothers. A male therapist may not be able to help the survivor reassess her family so that her anger and rage can be given to her perpetrator rather than to herself and her mother. Additionally he may minimize the perpetrator's responsibility for the sexual abuse and put some or all of the responsibility on the survivor. Recently a woman came to me for therapy after having been raped. The male therapist she saw prior to me asked her, "So what do you think your part was in the rape?" The woman, who was already feeling guilty and responsible, felt blamed for the sexual assault. Some men may also be aroused by the sexual details. Although this may also occur for a woman therapist, it is more frequent for male therapists to find the details erotic.

Spiritual therapists may want the survivor to forgive prematurely. The fact is that forgiveness is not a prerequisite for recovery and may never be appropriate. Yet therapists who have been influenced by a turn-the-other-cheek ideology or some other ideology of forgiveness may not recognize the client's need not to forgive.

These cautions about issues that may arise for the therapist are not insurmountable. But it is important that they be acknowledged as possibilities for the therapist working with sexual abuse survivors. Supervision by other therapists and consultants who are knowledgeable about incest recovery is extremely helpful. Issues of transference and countertransference are common in therapeutic alliances. Therefore, the opportunity to talk about these issues with a supportive, competent supervisor is essential.

Finally, there are many incest survivors who are themselves therapists working with sexually abused clients. For them, this work in particular can stir up issues that are very close. It is important that therapists who are survivors have a supportive network that can attend to them when feelings get restimulated. I suggest that the therapist who is a survivor be certain that she has actively worked on her own recovery process. It may be helpful for the survivor therapist, as well as the nonsurvivor therapist, to be involved in her or his own ongoing therapy.

SURVIVOR ISSUES

Additional issues that may come up when working with survivors of childhood sexual abuse include, in particular, body image, sex, family relationships, suicides, addictions and compulsions, and phobias.

In the United States culture, women generally have issues around body image. We are a culture that is obsessed with thinness and youth. For survivors, this may be a particularly difficult area because they have had their bodies stolen from them by their perpetrators. Survivors often develop body sizes as a form of protection. Some women who are anorexic or bulimic may view thinness as a way of protecting themselves from their abuse history, and others may overeat and use large body size as a way to feel safe. This area is addressed through directed activities that promote the client's acceptance of her body regardless of its size or shape. Identifying the issue of body size as a form of protection may help the survivor learn to let go of her protective strategy and feed herself according to her individual needs. This may result in a change in body size to one that is in sync with her body type and metabolism. Helping survivors learn to look at their bodies without judgment is a beginning step. Affirmations such as "I love myself unconditionally" may be added to the daily ritual of looking at her body. It is necessary to help the survivor understand that the perpetrator stole her body from her through his abuse, and to remind the survivor that our culture has given women unrealistic expectations about their bodies and that bodies naturally come in all different shapes and sizes. Finally, guided imagery, hypnosis, and structured activities that focus on self-acceptance can be useful.

Sex is another area that survivors often identify as a problem. Specific suggestions were discussed in chapters 10 and 11, but I remind therapists that this is an area they may need to identify for the survivor. Often survivors are embarrassed to discuss sex and the fact that it is a problem for them, and therefore they may not bring this topic up on their own. Identifying sex as a general area of concern for survivors may help the client discuss it more freely.

Family relationships, particularly differences between the survivor's family and her partner's family, may become a major area of conflict. Some survivors have reported that they find themselves being very jealous of their partner's relationship with his or her family, particularly if it is a positive one. A survivor may also feel upset by her partner's relationship to the survivor's family. If the partner is angry and wants nothing to do with the survivor's family, the survivor may feel resentful of her partner's relationship with his or her own family and of the fact that he or she does not want a relationship with the survivor's family. If the partner is friendly to the survivor's family, the survivor may feel abandoned and let down by her partner for his or her failure to take a stand against the survivor's family. Either one of these situations can result in major resentments, anger, and conflict.

Addictions and compulsions may also be issues for the survivor. Addictions, including drug, alcohol, and food addictions, need to be addressed in therapy. It is essential that the survivor get support and assistance in overcoming them. Alcoholics Anonymous, Narcotics

Anonymous, and Adult Children of Alcoholics are helpful resources, and in-patient rehabilitation may be necessary for some survivors who are addicted. Survivors who are actively alcohol- or drug-dependent should not be included in survivor groups. Additionally, newly recovering substance abusers may suffer relapses during the sexual abuse recovery period. Sobriety is essential, and therefore recovering addicts need to be involved in ongoing, supportive networks that focus on their addictions while they are engaged in individual sexual abuse recovery therapy.

As mentioned earlier, survivors may be actively suicidal during periods of recovery. Hospitalization must be considered an option if suicidal behavior escalates and there is danger of a completed suicide. For most survivors, suicidal thoughts can be handled without hospitalization. When I am working with clients who are suicide risks, I suggest a suicide contract in which the client agrees to call me before she acts on her suicidal thoughts, and I agree to be available by phone on a twenty-four-hour basis. I also use my relationship with the client, including my support and admiration for her, as a way of bolstering her through the crisis. *All* depressed clients need to be asked explicitly if they are feeling suicidal and if they have specific plans. I emphatically express to my clients that suicide is a bad idea and that all things can change but suicide. Death is irreversible!

Any phobias the survivor may have need to be addressed. I have known clients who have been immobilized and debilitated by phobias acquired from early childhood trauma—fears of being poisoned, of being closed in, of being watched, and so on. If the therapist does not feel confident in working on phobias, she or he may need to refer the client to a specialist in this area. Some therapists use hypnosis, desensitization, neurolinguistic programming, and other specialized techniques to deal with clients who have thought patterns that interfere with their functioning.

Although many areas can be problematic for the survivor of childhood sexual abuse, the above difficulties are quite common. The therapist would be wise to ask specifically about these areas; many clients have reported that having therapists acknowledge these difficult areas has been helpful in their recovery process.

CHAPTER THIRTEEN

Partners and Family of Creation

The trauma of childhood sexual abuse and the recovery process impact on the important people in the survivor's life. Partners, in particular, may find themselves being deeply affected by the survivor's healing journey. Some partners feel that their relationship was affected by the sexual abuse right from the beginning, whereas others state that everything seemed to be just fine and then all of a sudden things changed. Some partners state that their relationship was tumultuous and filled with crisis right from the start, whereas others state that a crisis seemed to develop out of nowhere. Whatever the case, sexual abuse recovery needs to be addressed by the partner.

There are issues that affect the survivor and her partner specifically, and the partner's response to these issues can help or hinder the recovery process. Sometimes the survivor acts out aggressively with her family of creation (her partner and/or children); she may be modeling the abuse that she learned as a child from her perpetrator and other family members, or she may be filled with rage and be displacing her anger onto her partner or her children. In either case, her behavior is extremely difficult and debilitating for both herself and her partner, and her partner's response is critical.

The partner must not engage in violent, abusive behavior with her. Many times, the survivor's violent outbursts may be headed off at the pass by asking the survivor what is going on or giving her space or an outlet for her anger before it escalates. Sometimes it may be necessary to restrain the survivor so that she doesn't hurt herself or others, but this must be done carefully. It is important that restraining her does not become a disguise for abusive behavior on the part of the partner. He or she needs to be honest about what is going on between them. Outside help needs to be obtained for the individuals and the couple. However, if there is battering in the relationship, couple therapy is not appropriate, as it implies that a couple can exist with battering and it places the battered person in risk of violence as a result of issues that arise in therapy; batterers' groups and individual therapy are more appropriate. Violence cannot be tolerated in any relationship. Abusive people can learn tools to control angry, violent outbursts—*feelings may not be controllable, but behavior is.* Batterers can learn to walk away, count to a thousand, leave the house, go for a jog, be alone to vent and scream—anything that will help stop the cycle of violence.

Sometimes survivors withdraw and isolate themselves. The partner may feel deserted and abandoned, especially if she or he has been accustomed to times when they seemed to do everything together. If the survivor has children and withdraws from them as well, the partner may have the additional burden of comforting the children during the survivor's retreat. During this period of isolation, numbness, and withdrawal, the survivor may fail to meet any or all of her other responsibilities as well. She may not work outside the home, cook, care for herself or her children, or function in any way, and her partner may have to take on these additional responsibilities. This may cause deep resentment and frustration. The partner may feel as if he or she is not being let into the survivor's life, that the survivor is detaching, and the partner may personalize what is happening, believing that the survivor is withdrawing because she no longer loves or needs him or her. Thus resentment and frustration are compounded by feelings of being unloved and unwanted.

Sex is often affected by the recovery process. Especially as the survivor and her partner are becoming family, sex may stir up intense emotions, panic attacks, and flashbacks. Some survivors may detach during sex, others may cry or scream when they have an orgasm, others may stop abruptly during lovemaking to escape flashbacks or intense feelings. These responses are difficult for the partner. It is difficult not to take them personally. Partners often report that they feel as if they are the abusers, because the survivor responds to them as if they were. It is tough to find oneself being treated as if one were abusive and fearsome.

It is important that the survivor not have sex unless she is willing. As mentioned in earlier chapters, it is important that the partner agree to the notion that they won't have sex unless the survivor wants to be sexual. There are times when it is most appropriate to be celibate. To insist on sexual involvement when the survivor does not want to be sexual is to replicate the abuse, and if the partner continues to pressure the survivor into having sex, in time the relationship will be affected not only by the childhood abuse but also by the abuse that is occurring in the present relationship. There are creative ways sexual issues can be worked out (see chapter 10).

Trust is often a problem for survivors, so it is not surprising that survivors have difficulty trusting their partners. This can be an extremely difficult area for the partner, who may feel misinterpreted and misunderstood. It is important that the partner understand that trust is bound to be a difficult area for the survivor, who was abused and not protected in childhood by people who were close to her. The survivor's feelings of mistrust were born in her childhood and have little or nothing to do with her current relationship, but since trust is an important ingredient in close relationships, it is no wonder that the partner is hurt and confused. However, partners can help build trust within the relationship by being trustworthy. The partner can begin with little steps, such as agreeing to perform a particular small task, like cooking dinner on Tuesdays or returning a library book for the survivor, and following through on the agreement. The promises can become bigger, such as keeping the survivor's confidence around a particular issue or spending the afternoon with the kids, and bigger, such as holding her without being sexual or participating in couple therapy with her. As commitments are made and kept, trust will begin to develop. It is important that the partner agree to commitments that he or she can and will keep.

Issues of control may also affect the couple. The survivor, who had no control as a child, may attempt to be very controlling now. She may attempt to make all the decisions that affect her and the couple. Control is very much a power issue, and the partner must remember that the survivor's need to control is based on her having been powerless as a child. Not to have control can make a survivor feel vulnerable and unsafe.

Power and control issues within couples can be worked out. Talking about them and how they affect the couple can be helpful. Letting the survivor know when she is being controlling may help her see it more clearly, and she may be able to give up some control as she feels safer within the relationship. Maintaining constant control can take up one's energy—energy that can be used for more helpful activities. Learning to share power and control with another can be freeing, and couple therapy may be very helpful in this area.

During sexual abuse recovery, the survivor feels intense emotions.

The partner may find that he or she is also experiencing intense emotions in response to what is happening in the couple's life. As mentioned in chapter 11, if both members of the couple are childhood sexual abuse survivors, all these emotions and responses to recovery may be multiplied because two people are going through them. Sometimes two survivors can give each other support. Other times, each one's recovery process stirs up overwhelming feelings and responses in the other. But whether couples include one or two survivors, each member of the couple will experience strong emotions as a result of the healing process, and more times than not they will be experiencing different emotions. In some cases this is helpful; the partner can respond appropriately to the survivor's feelings because they are different from the feelings the partner is experiencing. Yet at other times, the differences between them interfere; neither understands the other. Intense emotions are normal, but the partner as well as the survivor must have a way of releasing them.

As the survivor goes through different emotions and stages, her partner may find himself or herself having to adjust accordingly. Times of calm may alternate with times of crisis; just when the couple is feeling some tranquility, new emotional turmoil may arise. This can produce a roller coaster effect that leaves the partner further confused and alienated.

The survivor may also have periods of profound depression and suicidal gestures and thoughts. These are particularly scary times for those who care for and love the survivor. During these times, the partner needs to give the survivor reassurance that things will change and get better. He or she must also be in touch with the survivor's therapist and network, and inform them of her depression and her talk of suicide.

Clearly, during sexual abuse recovery, the survivor is not the only one who needs support—her partner needs emotional support as well. The partner needs to rev up his or her own network, which may include therapy, partners' groups, friends, and family. Therapy is a place to freely speak about the sexual abuse and its effect on the family's life. It is a place to express the resentment, anger, frustration, disappointment, shame, and fear one has about being a partner of a survivor. In utilizing the support of friends and family, it is important that the partner get permission from the survivor about what the partner can discuss concerning her abuse and recovery process.

During the stages of recovery, the partner may find himself or herself asking, "Where do I fit into this?" or "How can I help?" Partners can be very helpful to the survivor in her healing process by being understanding, empathetic, and supportive. However, totally denying his or her own needs can lead to resentment, anger, guilt, and withdrawal, so it is imperative that the partner take care of himself or herself. Besides getting the support of therapy and friends, the partner must take time for activities that are meaningful and enjoyable. If the partner and survivor used to engage in activities together and haven't done so in a while, it may be time for the partner to enjoy activities with others. Activities alone and with others can help maintain the partner's well-being during difficult times.

Partners may find themselves feeling responsible for the survivor's emotional responses. They may wonder what they did to elicit the survivor's reactions. The partner may try to make things better by diverting or entertaining the survivor. But the partner is not responsible for the abuse or the recovery process or the pain it might entail. The best thing a partner may be able to do is listen, respond to the survivor's need for company or space, or attend to the children. This can only happen without resentment and frustration if the partner takes care of himself or herself.

When there is a conflict of needs—which may happen often—the partner needs to decide what she or he can and cannot compromise. Open communication is important. The partner should express clearly what he or she needs and wants, knowing that the survivor is not obligated to fulfill the partner's desires. Each member of the couple has a right to ask for anything, but each member equally has the right to say no.

Problem-solving skills can be utilized to work out differences. First, each person needs to clearly define the problem. Following this, a brainstorming session should be held; all possible solutions—*without* evaluations—should be expressed. When the list is complete, each possible solution is judged for its merits and deficiencies. When they have all been evaluated, the couple may agree on which solution is most acceptable and when it can be implemented. Of course, sometimes a solution cannot be found; in that case, the conflict may be tabled for a while or brought up with a third party.

There may be times when compromises and solutions cannot be worked out. The partner and/or the survivor may rethink the relationship, and one or both may decide to separate. They may wish to consider this a temporary separation of several days or months or indefinitely, or they may wish the separation to be considered permanent. Working on recovery can be a very difficult process for the couple, and the decision to separate may seem like the only option. To end a relationship is not necessarily a failure. Sometimes the decision to separate is the right decision. In these cases, couple counseling can take on the task of helping the couple to separate successfully.

If the couple stays together and continues to grow, other difficulties may arise. If the partner is getting his or her needs fulfilled by being the "rescuer," he or she may feel threatened by the survivor's emotional growth. As the survivor becomes stronger and learns to take care of her own needs, her partner may feel left out and no longer needed. Support groups are particularly helpful for the partner who finds that he or she is feeling a loss at the survivor's newfound strength. Partners groups, Adult Children of Alcoholics, and Alanon may help the partner to discover the origin of his or her need to be a savior or co-dependent, and his or her own recovery work will enhance both the individuals and the couple (see the resources included in bibliography).

If the couple decides to remain together and to continue to struggle and grow, there are specific exercises that I suggest. The first is for each partner, without the other present, to make a list of the things that she or he loves about the other. After the lists are finished, they are to be read to one another. These lists need to be posted in a place that both members of the couple can see daily. When things get difficult—and they will—the partners can see why they love each other and why they are committed to staying together. There will be times when they have to be reminded of those reasons.

I also suggest that the partners make a commitment to spending quality time with each other, time when they can laugh together and be together. If the survivor is able to participate in activities, I suggest that they set aside a particular time each week—maybe an hour, maybe an afternoon, maybe an evening—in which they will be together without others. Each member of the couple takes a turn planning a fun activity. All couples need novelty as well as routine. Most couples are good on routine but not so good on novelty. This commitment gives the couple a chance to put novelty into their relationship on a regular basis.

Besides exercises for the couple to do, there are several activities that may be helpful to the partner. He or she may write a letter to the perpetrator and/or the survivor's family as a means of releasing anger and rage. This, like the letter that a survivor might write, is not meant to be sent, although it can be (with the survivor's permission), but rather is a catalyst for releasing pent up emotions.

Additionally I suggest that partners keep journals to record their reactions to and feelings about the recovery process. This records the developments of the couple and the individuals within the couple over a period of time, and this often helps the partner to recognize the gains made by the survivor, the partner, and the relationship.

Often I ask partners to make a gratitude list. This is a list of the beneficial things they get from being in a relationship with a survivor. Sometimes partners focus only on the couple's struggles and fail to notice the positive things that they gain from being involved with a woman who is actively working on incest recovery. Some benefits may include involvement in a relationship that is growing, openness with themselves and others, and involvement with someone who is brave and strong and loving.

Although things may get tough in a relationship that is dealing with childhood sexual abuse recovery, the recovery process is also a time when the bonds between partners can be strengthened. Even in the best relationship, there are as many reasons to leave as there are to stay. And although there is no right or wrong decision, staying and working on the relationship may result in a more loving, honest connection—one that grows stronger as time goes by.

CHAPTER FOURTEEN

Mothers

This is about mothers and for mothers. In this culture mothers are blamed for almost everything that goes wrong within a family. How often do we hear caseworkers, teachers, doctors, and other helping professionals respond to the knowledge of incest with the words, "How could that mother have let that happen?" We find it easier to get angry at mothers for not safeguarding their children than to get angry at perpetrators for raping children.

Survivors, too, often express great anger at their mothers for not having protected them from the perpetrators' abuse. As mentioned earlier, raging at the mother is often a necessary step in the recovery process.

As a therapist, I am aware of the survivor's need to rage at her mother. As a feminist, I am aware that patriarchal society creates a situation in which mothers are often powerless, depressed, and frustrated. It is essential to examine the role of mothers in both the pain and the healing of their daughters. To look at one without the other would paint a distorted picture of the role of mothers. The mother sometimes can be held responsible for failing to protect. More times than not, she was another victim in the family. But regardless of her position, we need to examine her role in the life of the child-victim and in the life of the adult-survivor. Mothers can be extremely helpful in the recovery process.

Mothers of survivors often wonder, "How can I help my daughter heal from the abuse?" and "How can I stop feeling guilty for my daughter's pain?"

Before answering these two questions, it may be helpful to examine the issues of responsibility and blame. What blame do mothers deserve, and what exactly are they responsible for? Mothers may be responsible for not protecting their daughters from abuse if in fact they were aware that the sexual and physical abuse was happening.

Some mothers were complicitous in their child's abuse and actively took part in it. Others were aware of the abuse and denied it either by not consciously acknowledging it or by knowing of it and just turning their heads. Some mothers were neglectful, frequently absent from home, or preoccupied with other issues in their lives. I know of mothers who left their children unattended because they were too drunk, too busy, too depressed, or too infatuated with a new romance to care for them. Some mothers were overtly abusive with their children—sexually, physically, or emotionally. Some clients have reported the severe beatings they received at the hands of their enraged mothers. Our culture blames mothers for the problems of their children, and sometimes mothers deserve the blame. More often than not, when mothers are neglectful or abusive, they are powerless and overwhelmed by life. They are women who are frustrated, depressed, overworked, and undervalued. This is not an excuse for their behavior but rather an explanation of the dynamics that may create a woman who abuses or neglects her children. Mothers can be held responsible for their neglectfulness and abusiveness. However, they are not to blame for the perpetrators' abuses.

Often mothers do not know of the sexual abuse of their children. In hindsight, they may look back and think that they should have known, but this is not always a fair assessment. Generally mothers do not suspect that their daughters are being abused because the father-perpetrator has worked hard to destroy the mother–daughter bond. With the bond severed, mothers are kept out of the lives of their daughters, and daughters do not see their mothers as sources of protection. The communication necessary for preventing or stopping sexual abuse does not exist. Since perpetrators do not usually sexually abuse children openly, mothers who are not told do not find out. Additionally, most women do not suspect that they have coupled with a child molester, so unless the abuse is overt, they don't suspect it's happening. Even in the case of overt abuse, denial is a strong defense mechanism that may keep the awareness of sexual abuse at bay.

As mentioned previously, fathers who sexually abuse their children have worked hard at severing the mother–daughter bond. They do this in several ways. In incestuous families, fathers often play the mother and daughter against each other. The father may do this by belittling the mother and by paying special attention to the daughter or by helping to create a role reversal between mother and daughter—treating his daughter like a wife and his wife like a child. One of my clients stated that when she was a child, at Christmastime her father bought her a gold bracelet and bought her mother a doll.

Incestuous fathers destroy the mother-daughter bond by being physically and emotionally abusive to the mother, giving her little or no economic power, and by completely dominating the family, so that everything has to be obtained through him. The children learn that the father has the power in the family and generally lose respect for the mother, who is seen as weak and powerless. When the father bestows attention, praise, and gifts on the daughter, she realizes that he is the only one who can be a source of comfort or protection. Even when the father is physically abusive to his daughter, he is still seen as the power broker in the family—the one who can make life miserable or bearable. A mother and daughter who have no power may become competitive for the resources the father controls. Is there any wonder that the daughter does not see her mother as a source of protection? Additionally, with the bond broken, even if she could protect her daughter, the mother generally does not have the relationship with her that would allow for her to learn that the abuse is occurring.

If the mother knows of the abuse and does nothing, it is often because she does not believe she is capable of stopping it. These are the mothers who see their spouses as their economic lifelines. They may not have or be able to obtain any money of their own; they may not be allowed to keep any of the money they earn. Such women are often physically and emotionally abused by their spouses as well, and their family histories generally show them to have been emotionally, physically, and/or sexually abused as children. They have not developed the economic or emotional tools necessary to protect themselves or their own children. They feel they cannot care for themselves or their children without the financial assistance of their partners. In the mind of such a woman, there is no alternative but to accept the abuse of herself and her children or face the seemingly impossible life of a single mother.

When the perpetrator is someone other than the father, the mother almost never is aware that her child is being sexually abused. If the sexual abuse is ongoing, the family system looks very similar to what was described above— domineering fathers and weak, powerless mothers. In some situations however, both the mother and father are emotionally unavailable and distant. The child may seek out the attention and company of the perpetrator or respond to his advances because she has been emotionally neglected. Without attention from her parents, she may misinterpret the sexual abuse as love and care.

When the sexual abuse is at the hands of a neighbor, teacher, doctor, friend of the family, or other person who may be seen as a surrogate family member or insider, the abuser often gives attention, praise, affection, and promises of love and devotion as ways of maintaining a hold on the victim. If the perpetrator is a grandfather, uncle, godfather, or another member of the extended family, the same dynamics may be in operation. The child sees the perpetrator as a source of attention and caring.

When a brother is the perpetrator, the child may see him as an ally against harsh or indifferent parents, or she may look up to him as a hero. In many cases, the brother is seen as powerful and frightening and the sister yields to his abusiveness out of fear. She may not tell because of violence or the threat of violence.

In the above cases, mothers may deserve blame for not protecting their daughters. They may deserve blame for being preoccupied, distant, or unavailable. They may deserve blame if they were complicitous, even if the cause was fear and powerlessness. *But mothers are not responsible for the abusive behavior of perpetrators.*

We also have many instances of mothers who have intervened—the sexual abuse of a daughter stopped when the mother found out about it. Mothers can be untapped sources of protection. I know of many cases in which mothers have actively and effectively protected their daughters once they learned of the abuse. I know of a mother who has been instrumental in educating parents, children, teachers, and the medical profession about child sexual abuse since learning of her children's abuse by a baby sitter. I know of another woman who gave herself and her daughters fifteen minutes to pack and move out of their home after learning of the sexual abuse by the children's father. Still other survivors report their mothers' roles in ending the sexual abuse through confrontation, separation, divorce, prosecution, and enforced family therapy. Mothers have been known to rise to the occasion and confront the menacing perpetrator.

Whether a mother knew about the sexual abuse or not, whether she later stopped the abuse or not, mothers of adult survivors ask how they can help their daughters through the recovery process. A mother can be a wonderful resource for her daughter during this period. It can be a difficult time for them both, but it can also be a time for mutual growth and respect. It can be a time to heal the mother-daughter bond and to create a stronger, more loving relationship.

When mothers first find out about the sexual abuse, a crisis develops. It is imperative that mothers get support. The survivor cannot be a source of support, as she is dealing with her own crisis. Individual therapy or a mothers' group can be essential in providing the needed guidance.

Once the mother has been told, first and foremost she must believe that the sexual abuse happened. Even if the perpetrator is someone the mother loves—a husband, a father, a brother, a son—she must be willing to let go of denial. This may be the most difficult task of all, because it may mean severing an important relationship with a loved one. If the family member/perpetrator denies the abuse, the mother will probably feel conflicted, torn between her daughter and the perpetrator. However, it is essential that she believe the survivor. If the perpetrator is her son, the mother usually feels guilty on two fronts—guilty for not protecting her daughter and guilty for her son's abusive behavior.

Once the mother learns of the abuse and believes it, it is essential that she tell her daughter that she is sorry that the daughter was hurt and abused. The mother can ask the survivor how she can be helpful to her in her recovery process. She can ask explicitly what her daughter wants and needs her to do. But it is important for the mother to understand that while the survivor can ask for anything, she herself can only do what she is capable of doing. This may be a time of bitterness and anger for the survivor, and she may ask for what seems impossible. If the mother cannot or will not do what is being asked, she must tell her daughter that although she wants to assist her, she is not able to meet her request. However, the mother can also tell her daughter what she can do to help. She may be able to financially support her during the immediate crisis of recovery, assist her with her children, get involved in family therapy, accept her path of recovery, or follow her cues regarding closeness and space.

If the mother wants to confront the perpetrator, she needs to get the survivor's permission. The survivor alone must decide if and when the perpetrator will be confronted and by whom. However, the mother can decide to sever the relationship with the perpetrator whether the survivor chooses a confrontation or not. The decision to maintain her relationship with the perpetrator rests with her. Although survivors often wish that their mothers would end relationships with perpetrators, they cannot make this decision for them. The mother may choose not to break off the relationship, particularly if it is with a husband or son. However, if the relationship between the mother and the perpetrator continues, it needs to change in some way to support the daughter's recovery process. This may include involving the perpetrator in family therapy or marital therapy, monitoring the perpetrator's involvement with children, and when necessary, going to court.

If a confrontation is planned, the mother needs to find out what her role is to be. Does the survivor want the mother at the confrontation? Does the survivor want other family members present? What is the survivor's expectation of her mother during the confrontation? If possible, the mother should agree to support her daughter's requests regarding the confrontation. In taking on a supportive role, especially around confrontation, and uniting with her daughter around this difficult task, the mother may not only promote her daughter's healing but also empower herself. This may be an opportunity for both mother and daughter to seize power. Although a confrontation may be scary and emotionally charged, it can bring mother and daughter closer by beginning to heal the mother–daughter bond.

In addition to the decision about confrontation, the survivor also decides whether or not other family members or friends will be told. Although the mother may wish to tell others, it is not her decision. Robin recalled how her mother's disclosure to extended family members affected her. "My mother decided she needed to fill in other family members, which I was not excited about. She told without my knowledge—against my wishes. If they [family members] have issues with my father, they don't need my issues. I don't want people disliking him because they're feeling sorry for me." Unless a mother has explicit permission from the survivor to talk to others about the abuse and recovery process, she should only utilize confidential resources, such as a therapist or a mothers' support group.

As mentioned earlier, the knowledge that one's daughter was sexually abused as a child brings on many emotions. In many ways, the mother's emotional responses may be identical to the daughter's. She may follow a path from denial, through depression, guilt, anger, and sadness, to letting go.

When she acknowledges that the sexual abuse happened (and the sooner her acknowledgment, the better, for both herself and the survivor), the mother may feel a combination of depression and guilt. To be most helpful to the survivor, *the mother must forgive herself.* Guilt cannot change the past. The important thing is that she is in a posi-

tion to be there for her daughter now. She must seize this opportunity. Additionally, she must forgive her daughter for being a child who
was powerless. Regardless of the perpetrator's accusations or rationalizations, the mother must remember that the sexual abuse was not
the survivor's fault.

The mother needs to release her anger. Like her daughter, as a
woman in this culture, the expression of anger may be difficult for
her. A therapist and/or support group can be helpful. It is likely that
the mother, too, did not have good role models for the expression of
anger. She, too, may need help in learning to express anger in an
appropriate manner. Like the survivor and the survivor's partner, the
mother may find it helpful to release her anger and rage by writing to
the perpetrator a letter that she may or may not send. She may also
engage in other anger-releasing exercises (see chapter 9).

After her anger passes, the mother may feel profound sadness. She
may feel sorrowful about her daughter's lost childhood, their strained
relationship, her lost relationship with the perpetrator or other family
members, and so on. During this time the mother needs to be reminded of her own good qualities. It may be helpful for her to make a list of
her noble qualities, such as honesty, fairness, compassion, or kindness,
or to make a list of her accomplishments, such as being there for her
adult daughter, being able to ask for help, or perhaps being able to ask
for forgiveness. This may also be a time for her to write a letter to her
daughter expressing her pride in and appreciation of her. It may be
helpful for her to tell her children that she loves them.

As the mother continues to respond to her daughter's sexual
abuse recovery, both mother and daughter may decide to spend quality time with each other. This may include intimate talks or outings
together. This needs to be agreed upon by both the survivor and the
mother. The survivor may need to keep her distance from her mother
or other family members during the healing process. As difficult as
that may be for her, the mother needs to respect her daughter's wishes regarding closeness and distance. In time their relationship may
evolve to a place that is mutually satisfying for both of them.

Being a mother is a tough job, one that is mythologized as being
respected and valued but in actuality gets little support in our patriarchal society. Mothers, particularly in traditional families, have little
power and much frustration. They are often held captive in abusive
family systems. Yet in the eyes of their young children, mothers loom
large and are expected to protect their children from all harm.

In spite of loving their children, mothers sometimes are not able to properly take care of them. Yet even if a mother has missed her opportunity to nurture and protect her young daughter, she may get an opportunity to help the adult daughter heal from sexual abuse. When a survivor gives her mother another chance to demonstrate her love by being there for her, she has given her mother a wonderful present. When the mother responds lovingly and appropriately, both the mother and the daughter receive a gift.

CHAPTER FIFTEEN

Others

Childhood sexual abuse recovery affects all the important people in the survivor's life. Although the effects may seem more obvious with a partner and mother, siblings, children, father, and friends may all be affected. The following discussion is meant as a guideline for the other important people within the survivor's network.

All the adults in the survivor's life can be helpful by listening to her, believing her, and supporting her decisions as they relate to her recovery—therapy, confrontations, disclosures, living arrangements, work choices, need for closeness and distance, and so on. It is also helpful for the survivor to hear explicitly that the support people in her life are sorry that she had to experience the sexual abuse.

The special dynamics of the various people in the survivor's life are discussed below. But besides discussing ways these individuals can be helpful, I also address the issues that affect them based on their relationship to her and suggest some ways the survivor can deal with her children during and after her recovery—whether they are still in her care or on their own.

SIBLINGS

Siblings can be both a comfort and a source of struggle for the survivor. Siblings who were also abused may have similarities and differences with the survivor. In some cases, the abused sibling may not want to actively engage in the recovery process and therefore may see her or his sister as a catalyst for pain. The survivor may be interfering with the sibling's decision to remain in denial. The sibling may ask, "Why are you bringing this up now? Let the past be the past." Such a reaction can be a source of pain for both the survivor and the sibling. Annette, whose parents are dead, talked about her current relationship with her sister. "She tries to be friendly, but I find her cold and remote. We're alienated. I went to visit her last Rosh Hashana, and we were having a conversation in which I said certain things from my past still affect me. And she, almost bordering on hysteria, said, 'Well, I'm sorry that my father was an alcoholic, and I'm sorry that my mother was a martyr. And I'm sorry that you were molested. But these things are all in the past. And after I got married, I made my own life and I forgot them.' Book was closed! The book was closed!"

Sometimes, the sibling is also actively working on recovery and may welcome the opportunity to share this process with her or his sister. They may be able to take comfort in each other's knowledge that something did in fact happen. They may be able to help each other reconstruct their childhoods in a way that helps them to have a clearer understanding of what they were like. Although there may be times when they have different needs because of their different places in the recovery process, with openness and respect siblings can work out these differences.

When the sibling was not abused or has no memory of being abused, some difficulties may arise. For instance, some nonabused siblings feel guilty for having been spared the abuse. Others, particularly older siblings, may feel guilty for not having protected the survivor. They cannot accept the fact that they, too, were children and were powerless to stop the perpetrator. But it is true; they could not protect the child victim. In the case of siblings who witnessed the sexual abuse, they, too, were victims.

In some cases, nonabused siblings may have resented the survivor because the survivor was seen as the "chosen one." The siblings may have felt rejected and unwanted because they were spared sexual involvement, which they may have perceived as love rather than abuse. In some cases, feelings of resentment and rejection last long after the sibling discovers the abusive nature of the relationship between the perpetrator and the survivor. This may be compounded by guilt for feeling such things. Margaret, age forty, explained that her sister was jealous and hostile because of the relationship between Margaret and her abusive father. "If only she knew what she was jealous about." Although feeling resentful and jealous of an abusive relationship may be difficult to understand, the perceived specialness of the relationship may distort the sibling's perception.

Several years ago, I began working with a woman who repeatedly witnessed her older brother raping her younger sister. Because witnessing molestation and rape is also a way of being sexually abused, the woman was in fact an incest survivor. I said to her, as I say to all my survivor clients, that I would not hit her, harm her, or have sex with her. I noticed that she gave a seemingly embarrassed laugh at my statement but declined to comment on it. Months later she explained to me that her laughter had been a reaction to rejection. She said, "I thought to myself, 'Well, I guess I'm not chosen again.'" Part of our work together has focused on her jealousy and her guilt about the jealousy as she successfully works on healing her relationship with her younger sister.

In spite of the obstacles mentioned above, siblings can be a wonderful source of support and comfort during the incest recovery process. They can help validate and verify specifics of the childhood abuse, and in some cases siblings are the only sources of the information that may help the survivor regain her memories. An empathetic, caring sibling can provide an amazing amount of relief during the healing process. She or he can become the much-needed shelter in the sometimes turbulent journey to recovery. Many survivors have reported that their siblings have been helpful to them not only in providing information and facts but also in validating their emotional responses to other family members.

Siblings can be helpful to the survivor in many ways. But before they can be helpful, they must forgive themselves for not having protected the survivor from the abuse. Additionally, they must acknowledge to themselves their feelings about the sexual abuse and their childhood. Admitting to the survivor that they may have felt resentment or jealousy, rather than denying those aspects of themselves, can help them to honestly engage in the recovery process with their sibling, although this admission should probably not be made during the initial stages of recovery. However, after the emotional crises diminish, openly expressing the feelings they had in childhood, and have at present, may open the door to enhanced communication and a closer relationship. Timing is very important. The sibling who genuinely wants to be helpful to the survivor needs to honestly assess her or his motivation before expressing opinions and feelings that may be upsetting. Admitting these feelings to oneself and to an objective third person before talking about them to the survivor may be beneficial.

If the sibling is feeling resentful, jealous, unlovable, or ambivalent, it will be helpful for her or him to remember that the sexual abuse was not the fault of the child-victim. Even if the relationship with the perpetrator seemed to have secondary gains for the survivor, it was still harmful and abusive. Special attention, gifts, and rewards were not worth the damage and injury inflicted upon the child.

It is also helpful for the sibling to remember that the sexual abuse was not her or his fault, either. Children are not to blame for the behavior of older, more powerful children or adults. Outside help, such as individual therapy, childhood sexual abuse survivor literature, or support groups, may be helpful in sorting out these feelings.

FATHERS (WHO WERE NOT PERPETRATORS)

Fathers, like mothers, have powerful effects on their children, even if only as the result of their having been absent or uninvolved. Yet fathers are often spared the wrath that is given to mothers. This may be because they are not expected to be sources of comfort or nurturance for their children. They are rarely seen as primary caretakers and may therefore be saved from the unrealistic expectations that are so often placed on mothers.

Fathers can still play positive, important roles in the lives of their children. Though it is more the exception than the rule, fathers can and have taken on the role of nurturer and protector. This may become less exceptional as feminism and the women's movement continue to challenge the culture to reevaluate gender roles and the structure of the nuclear family.

In the case of incestuous families and families in which sexual abuse by friends and neighbors has affected one or more of the children, certain patterns of fatherhood can be seen. In such families, fathers are usually domineering. Though not the perpetrators of sexual abuse, they are often physically and/or emotionally abusive. Phyllis, who was abused by her older brother, described her father. "He was emotionally abusive to my mother, brother, and me. He was always angry, and we were all afraid of him. As early as I can remember, we did not have a good relationship. We'd all be waiting for his business trips so the house would be more relaxed. My brother—we were comrades in alliance against my father."

Ellen, who was abused by several friends of the family, told of her mother's fear of her father. "My mother was intimidated by him [father], too. I would sit on her lap. And he'd say, 'None of this lovey-dovey shit, get her off your lap.' And she would—at three or four."

Her younger sister, Joan, who is thirty-nine and was also abused by the same family friends, described the dynamics of her family. "We were five people who lived in the house, and we each had our own separate rooms. And my life was outside with my animals and in the bedroom. And I would go down for meals. And that would be the extent of our interaction. No interaction except that my father would lecture. I don't remember ever talking to my mother about anything. She was always overwhelmed, harried, and distracted."

In some cases, fathers of sexually abused children are not abusive or tyrannical but instead are emotionally absent and neglectful. Being emotionally distant may be a direct result of our cultural expectation that men not cultivate their tender side. Additionally, the gender role expectation of men to be the breadwinners may force them to devote their time and energy to their careers and leave the caretaking role to the mother. But regardless of the reasons for it, the father's distance can leave his daughter vulnerable to sexual abuse, particularly by attentive outsiders such as neighbors, teachers, and friends of the family. Although in most cases fathers didn't mean to fail their children, their failure to be warm, nurturing, and communicative left their daughters vulnerable to sexual abuse.

When a father who is not the perpetrator learns of the sexual abuse of his daughter, he may feel emasculated and see himself as having failed in his role as family protector. He may feel embarrassed, guilty, and defeated. He may initially feel more upset for himself than for his daughter and see the sexual abuse of his daughter as a personal affront to him, for in our patriarchal culture, children are seen as the possessions of the father. However, after this initial self-pity, most fathers feel upset for the pain of their daughters.

Not all fathers of survivors fit the above description. Some fathers have attempted to be loving and caring of their offspring, yet their children have been sexually abused. They, like many mothers, have not contributed to the sexual abuse risk of their children. In these cases, the sexual abuse is generally reported to someone (usually a family member) soon after the abuse begins. It is in the case of ongoing sexual abuse that the above-described dynamics usually exist.

Whether fathers were physically and emotionally abusive or not, whether they were distant and neglectful or not, they can assist their daughters through the sexual abuse recovery process. The current relationship can be warm and caring regardless of past mistakes. Fathers who did not abuse their children, like mothers and siblings, need to forgive themselves for their past errors. They can make up for their past mistakes by giving the survivor assistance and comfort now. Fathers can learn to be open, affectionate, trustworthy, and responsive to the needs of their children.

FRIENDS

Friends are not unaffected by the survivor's recovery process. Many times survivors turn to their friends for support, rather than to their families, because they feel closer to them. Survivors may think of friends as the family of choice, while they see their actual family as the result of an accident of birth. Friends may be extremely helpful and able to give love and support in ways the survivor's family cannot.

Friends are not affected by the survivor's history in the same way that family members are, particularly with respect to the issue of not having protected the survivor, yet intense feelings can still be aroused. Sometimes the survivor is very open with her friends about the sexual abuse and talks frequently about the childhood trauma and its effects on her. She may talk about her recovery process constantly to the exclusion of other topics. She may seem obsessed with the incest and no longer interested in the activities she and her friends previously enjoyed together. As a result, her friends may feel abandoned. They may at times feel overwhelmed by the survivor's devotion to her recovery process and find themselves confused and burdened. Yet in spite of these feelings, it will be helpful if friends understand that the survivor must do whatever she needs to do to work on her recovery.

Sometimes the survivor may withdraw from her friends as she submerges herself in the recovery process. She may withdraw because she thinks she must hide her "secret" from her friends, believing that they will not understand or that they will think less of her. While actively engaged in the recovery process, she may feel more of an alliance with other survivors than with her old friends. Again, the result may be that her friends feel left out and abandoned.

Friends can be most helpful if they respect the survivor's process, be there for her when they are needed, and support her attempts to take care of herself. Sometimes the most important thing a friend can do for a survivor is to watch the survivor's children and assure her that they will be attended to during this difficult process.

Friends, old and new, may be the network the survivor turns to during emotional crisis. She may reach out to them when she is feeling overwhelmed. However, it may also happen that when she needs her friends the most, she withdraws from them. If she becomes depressed and suicidal, she may recoil from life and be unable to reach out. Phone calls, notes and cards, visits, and encouragement from her friends can be very helpful.

Friends can help the survivor get through difficult periods in the recovery process. Even if the survivor is involved in therapy, is reuniting with her family of origin, and has a supportive, loving partner, her strong friendships can be the catalyst for the survivor to utilize all of her resources. In many ways, friends are in a unique position to help her. They are close enough to understand and love the survivor, yet they may be objective enough not to be threatened by the survivor's needs and wants during this emotionally charged period.

CHILDREN

Children of survivors are often the least understood and the least discussed of all people touched by the survivor's recovery process. Yet in many ways they are more affected than anyone, except the survivor herself, by that process.

As mentioned earlier, survivors may first recall their incest history because of trigger points, events that trigger a memory. Many times their own children have had this effect. Trigger points have included the birth of a baby, a child reaching the age when the survivor was first sexually assaulted, a child's interaction with the perpetrator. Sometimes the sexual abuse of her own child brings on the survivor's memories. When children are the catalysts for the survivor's awareness of her incest history, the relationship between the survivor and her child may be strained. Even when the child has no connection to the survivor's childhood memories, the survivor for a time may have difficulties caring for her children.

Sometimes as the recovery process evolves, the survivor is unable to attend to her children. She may be depressed and withdrawn and unable to cope with her children's needs with the energy that they require. She may be feeling angry and enraged, and she may displace this fury onto her children. Though she does not intend to harm them, she may be neglectful or abusive because she is unable to cope with them. When this happens, *it is imperative that the survivor get assistance!* She is not "bad" for being unable to care for her children, but she must be certain that they are provided for, or she also will be guilty of abuse. This is a time when friends, family members, partners, social service agencies, and childcare agencies can be essential.

The survivor needs to explain to her children that she is an incest survivor and that she is working on healing from the abuse. Children should be told in language they can understand—without overexplaining or underexplaining. A small child might be told, "Grandpa hurt me when I was small. Sometimes I get sad when I remember it. I'm not mad at you. I'm angry at Grandpa." Older children can hear phrases like *sexually abused, incest,* or *molested* in the explanation but do not need to hear specific details of the abuse. The purpose of telling the child about the survivor's abuse and current state is to assure the child that she or he didn't do anything wrong and is not responsible for her or his mother's state. Children generally pick up that things are wrong but often misinterpret and believe that they are the cause for the difficulties. This may also be an opportunity to talk to children about sexual abuse prevention issues, such as being in charge of their bodies, being able to say no, and telling if anyone talks to or touches them in a way that makes them uncomfortable. (Books on this topic are listed in the bibliography.)

By explaining to her children on an appropriate level that she was abused and that she is working on feeling better, the survivor can assuage her children's fears that they will be abandoned, can explain why they may be in the care of others for a while, and can assure them that they are not to blame. This is a time to remind the children that they are good and strong and loved.

This may also be a time when the child can be helpful to the survivor by learning to listen and give comfort. Sometimes it is okay to let the child be helpful. However, it's important that roles are not reversed. The mother is still the grown-up and her daughter or son is still a child. If the survivor cannot take on these parental responsibilities, including the children's care, she needs assistance in providing for their well-being. Survivors who need help in caring for their children and can ask for it are to be commended for their strength and courage.

Grown children, although no longer dependent on the survivor, can also be affected by their mother's recovery process. They, too, need to know what's happening if their mother's emotional state or behavior has changed. Even when they are no longer living with her, children are often keenly aware of their mother's emotional and physical well-being. This may be an opportunity for the adult child to be supportive and consoling. Like the other adults in the survivor's life, the grown child can listen and give encouragement as the survivor continues on her path of recovery. If their adult connection is a continuation of an open and loving relationship, this will be an opportunity to further deepen their bond. If their relationship has had a history of turmoil and distance, the survivor runs the risk of not receiving support and maybe even of widening the gap. On the other hand, this may be an opportunity for the survivor and her grown children to begin setting the stage for a more open and communicative relationship. It may be the beginning of a more mutually respectful and loving connection.

Disclosure to children is a question not only for survivors who are in early stages of recovery. Survivors who have emerged from earlier emotionally charged stages or have made it to the letting-go stage, may wonder whether to discuss their incest histories with their children. I believe that it is important to discuss one's incest history with adolescent and adult children.

Mothers often relay implicit messages to their children about men in general or their perpetrator in particular, as a result of their being incest survivors. It is important to be clear with children and to make sure that they are understanding the messages that are being relayed. Since messages are given, they might as well be explicit. For instance, when a mother intentionally or unintentionally gives her children subtle messages about the dangers of involvement with men but does not give them a clear understanding of her history, children may develop a generalized distrust of men. For girls, that can result in a fear of men. For boys, it can result in a fear that they themselves are untrustworthy. By talking about her incest history, a mother allows her children to understand what her beliefs are based on and to know that they can use this information in conjunction with their own experiences to make their own assessments of the world.

Another reason to disclose is because hiding this aspect of oneself reinforces the belief that one's sexual abuse history is somehow shameful. Disclosing also prevents the chance of having the "secret" told to them by someone else.

Frances, forty-three years old, emerged to the letting-go stage but had not told her son that she had been sexually abused by her father. While Frances was in the midst of a divorce from her husband,

George, he threatened to tell their son, fourteen years old at the time, in order to pressure her to make come concessions in the divorce agreement. Had Frances talked to her son about her history, George would not have had this opportunity to attempt to blackmail her.

Finally, openly discussing one's incest history with one's children gives them an opportunity to better understand their mother, learning of her strengths and courage.

Sexual abuse recovery work has a profound impact on the survivor and her relationships. The support and encouragement of the adults in the survivor's life may be instrumental in bolstering her confidence and trust, things that were so badly damaged when she was victimized as a child. When a survivor opens up about her recovery process, she is taking a giant step. She is taking a chance on the people in her life. When the important people in her life respond with kindness, encouragement, empathy, and support, they open the way for the survivor to make deep, loving connections—a necessary ingredient for living a fulfilling and empowering life.

CHAPTER SIXTEEN

Conclusion

The discussion of incest survivors and their recovery process speaks not of conclusions but rather of beginnings. The journey from victim to survivor does not end there. Healing from childhood sexual abuse allows the survivor to go from surviving to thriving.

My work with incest survivors has been inspiring. I have witnessed the enormous growth of women who were demoralized and brutalized as children as they emerge as strong, capable, loving women. It seems no less miraculous than watching a butterfly emerge from its cocoon. The privilege of working with incest survivors has demonstrated to me the tremendous capabilities of the human spirit, particularly the spirit of women.

In working with incest survivors I have learned not only what is helpful to their recovery but also what hinders the process. There are certain pitfalls that therapists, physicians, teachers, partners, friends, and other support persons need to avoid. Behaviors and attitudes that are not helpful to the child-victim or the adult-survivor include minimizing the sexual abuse, denying it, not respecting the survivor's healing process, and accepting the notion that sex between an adult and a girl is not alarming.

Patricia, a social worker in a child protection unit, spoke of the reaction of some of her co-workers to the victimization of girls. "When a boy is victimized by his father, everyone wants to lock the father up. They're more irate. Staff say, 'He should be castrated.' They are much more tolerant of father–daughter incest."

Candace, age forty-two, recalled her first therapist's reaction. "I told a male therapist in college about it [incest] and he said 'I don't think that is an issue.' I went back into silence for two more years."

Barbara explained how the reactions from teachers hurt her. "Being labeled as a weird kid when I tried to communicate in the ways that I knew how—which were pretty cryptic. Teachers were distressed about me masturbating in class and some other stuff I did which I think was pretty connected to the abuse."

Not only individual behaviors hinder the recovery process; the cultural view that devalues women and children promotes an environment inimical to thriving. Children in particular are seen as possessions of the men in their lives. What feminist researchers have pointed out—that the exploitation of women and children is condoned in religious law (Rush, 1980) and protected by our legal and medical system (Herman, 1981, 1984)—is distinctly known by incest survivors. Incest survivors know that the men who sexually abused them were ordinary men—men who were generally respected in their communities. Incest survivors know that the power relationships in the family and in society are heavily tilted in favor of men, and that women and children hold little power in relationship to men. Armed with this knowledge, many incest survivors are working to make themselves independent, strong, and whole.

My work with incest survivors has taught me what is helpful in the healing process. There is no formula for healing, but there is a developmental process. However, the specific steps are not always the same for all survivors. Some survivors confront their perpetrators, others do not. Some survivors have bonded with their mothers, others have not. Some survivors remain in the same towns as their families, others move clear across the continent to get away from their families. No matter what action is taken by the survivor, healing is related directly to her individual work, not to the actions of the perpetrator. Regardless of the specific steps, the recovery pattern is a developmental process that includes introspection, such as acknowledging the abuse and working through intense emotions, followed by an action, such as renegotiating family patterns or involvement in a survivor's mission.

Additionally I have learned that there is no such thing as one form of childhood sexual abuse being worse than another. Whether the sexual abuse is seductive and manipulative or violent and sadistic, it is harmful and profoundly affects the survivor. Severity of sexual violence does not necessarily affect the recovery rate. In fact, seductive sexual abuse that includes secondary gains of attention, rewards, and gifts often leaves the survivor believing that she was complicitous and feeling guilty, which can complicate the recovery process. Violent, brutal abuse may allow the survivor to more easily understand that she was not a willing party to it. Regardless of the specifics of the childhood sexual abuse, all incest is traumatic.

Although the survivor is the principal character in the recovery process, friends, partners, family members, therapists, and other helping professionals can assist. We must bear witness, validate her experiences and emotions, be empathetic, and be respectful of her process. We must honor her coping mechanisms and see them as survival behaviors. The survivor may discover that some of her survival skills are no longer needed and replace them with more helpful tools. She may decide that some of them are necessary for her continued safety and growth. We, as supporters of her recovery, must recognize that the survivor is the ultimate expert on what she needs to do to proceed.

Survivors have healed from childhood sexual abuse in many ways. Some have used individual therapy and incest survivors' groups, some have used the arts, such as painting, photography, sculpturing, writing. Some women have nourished their spirituality by becoming involved in twelve-step programs, or the study of Wicca (a goddess religion), by modifying traditional religious beliefs in a way that promotes feelings of inner strength and well-being as women and survivors, or by finding ways to experience greater connections to nature and the universe. Most incest survivors I have interviewed identify a survivor's mission as an essential part of their healing process. This may include counseling battered women, working with abused and neglected children, organizing an incest speakout, working in child abuse prevention programs, writing poetry for other survivors. Any way of making their incest recovery a gift has been a catalyst for growth.

There is one more step in this process: the recognition that being an incest survivor is only one aspect of the whole person. Being a survivor is an important and strong part of the whole, but it is only a part. In time, the survivor needs to cultivate all her parts. She must recognize that she is more than her history. She needs to understand that she is the architect of her future. She is in charge now!

There is one character who is missing from this story—the perpetrator. I have chosen not to include him for many reasons. First and foremost, he has had enough power and attention, and I do not wish to give him any more. Additionally, although I have researched their pathology, I choose not to work with perpetrators. I believe that in order to work effectively with a client, one must empathize with her or him. I do not want to empathize with perpetrators. Although some survivors forgive their perpetrators, I do not want the role of explaining or presenting the perpetrator's side of the story, or to encourage or discourage any decision the survivor might make about him.

This is a book about women who are recovering from incest and the people who support them. It is about hope and strength. Margaret summarized the recovery process. "I have done a tremendous amount of work on myself in therapy, with spirituality, attending workshops. I have opportunities to abuse my kid, but I don't and won't. The buck stops here. . . . The payoff has been gradual, but I see a progression throughout my adult life. . . . I'm healthier and healthier, happier and happier."

REFERENCES

Armstrong, L. (1982). The cradle of sexual politics: Incest. In M. Kirkpatrick (Ed.), *Women's sexual experience: Explorations of the dark continent.* New York: Plenum Press.

Barry, K., Bunch, C., & Castley, S. (1984). *Networking against female sexual slavery.* New York: The International Women's Tribune Centre.

Bates, C. M., & Brodsky, A. M. (1989). *Sex in the therapy hour: A case of professional incest.* New York: Guilford Press.

Bass, E., & Davis, L. (1988). *The courage to heal.* New York: Harper & Row.

Biale, R. (1984). *Women and Jewish law.* New York: Schocken Books.

Butler, S. (1978). *Conspiracy of silence: The trauma of incest.* San Francisco: Volcano Press.

Butler, S. (1986, September). Creativity, community, and healing. Presented at Albany Rape Crisis Center's Conference on Sexual Abuse, Albany, N.Y.

Dworkin, A. (1974). *Woman hating.* New York: E. P. Dutton.

Freud, S. (1962). The aetiology of hysteria. In J. Strachey (Ed.) *The Standard Edition of the Complete Works of Sigmund Freud.* Volume 3. London: Hogarth Press.

Goleman, D. (1989, August 15). Brain's design emerges as a key to emotions. *New York Times,* C: 1, 9.

Groth, A. N. (1979). *Men who rape: The psychology of the offender.* New York: Plenum Press.

Groth, A. N., & Sgroi, S. (1986, June). Child sexual abuse: Victims, offenders, and survivors. Presented at the Massachusetts Forensic Mental Health Child Abuse Conference, Dedham, MA.

Herman, J. (1982). *Father–daughter incest.* Cambridge, MA: Harvard University Press.

Herman, J. (1984). *Work in Progress.* No. 83–05. Wellesley, MA: Wellesley College.

Herman, J. (1986, October). Keynote address at University of Wisconsin Conference on Sexual Abuse, Madison, WI.

Hirschmann, J. R., & Munter, C. H. (1989). *Overcoming overeating.* New York: Fawcett.

Keyes, K. (1981). *The Hundredth Monkey.* St. Mary, KY: Vision Books.

Kübler-Ross, E. (1969). *On death and dying.* New York: MacMillan.

Lerner, H. G. (1985). *The dance of anger.* New York: Harper & Row.

Loulan, J. (1987). *Lesbian passion: Loving ourselves and each other.* San Francisco: Spinsters/Aunt Lute Book Company.

Malamuth, N. M. (1981). Rape proclivity among males. *Journal of Social Issues, 37* (4): 138–157.

Roth, G. (1985). *Breaking free from compulsive eating.* New York: MacMillan.

Rush, F. (1980). *The best kept secret: Sexual abuse of children.* Englewood Cliffs, NJ: Prentice Hall.

Russell, D. (1982). *Rape in marriage.* New York: MacMillan.

Russell, D. (1986). *The secret trauma: Incest in the lives of girls and women.* New York: Basic Books.

SELECTED ANNOTATED BIBLIOGRAPHY

CHILDHOOD SEXUAL ABUSE LITERATURE: By Survivors

Bass, E., & Thornton, L. (Eds.) (1983). *I never told anyone: Writings by women survivors of child sexual abuse*. New York: Harper & Row.

This anthology includes writings by survivors of childhood sexual abuse by family members, acquaintances, and strangers.

Brady, K. (1979). *Father's day*. New York: Dell.

This is an autobiographical account of father–daughter incest in which the author describes her childhood survival skills and the later life effects of the sexual abuse.

Hill, E. (1985). *The family secret: A personal account of incest*. New York: Dell.

This autobiographical account of father–daughter incest reflects the patterns often found in incestuous families, the ambivalence and conflicts often felt by the child-victim and the adult-survivor, and the life patterns that may result from childhood sexual abuse.

McNaron, T., & Morgan, Y. (Eds.) (1982). *Voices in the night: Women speaking about incest*. San Fransisco: Cleis Press.

This anthology of prose, poetry, rituals, and essays emerged from an ongoing lesbian writers' group. Although most of the writings are about abuse by men, a few accounts of sexual abuse by women are included.

Randall, M. (1987). *This is about incest*. Ithaca, NY: Firebrand Books.

Through the use of poetry, collage, and prose, Randall details her healing journey from the effects of incestuous abuse by her grandfather.

SEXUAL ABUSE LITERATURE

Armstrong, L. (1978). *Kiss daddy goodnight*. New York: Pocket Books.

This book, through the use of survivors' words and the author's analysis, details the effects of childhood sexual abuse and later life effects of the abuse. This is one of the earlier accounts of incest from a nonclinical population and is an example of feminism's early influence on research.

Armstrong, L. (1982). The cradle of sexual politics: Incest. In M. Kirkpatrick (Ed.), *Women's sexual experience: Explorations of the dark continent*. New York: Plenum Press.

This is a thorough and wonderful historical account of attitudes toward incest, beginning with Freud's denial through family systems theory to the pro-incest contingent.

Armstrong, L. (1989). *Solomon says: A speakout on foster care*.

This is an indictment of our foster care system, exposing how the social service bureaucracy damages children, including those who enter the system because of sexual abuse.

Bass, E., & Davis, L. (1988). *Courage to heal*. New York: Harper & Row.

This is a wonderful resource book for survivors of childhood sexual abuse.

Blake-White, J., & Kline, C. M. (1985). Treating dissociative process in adult victims of childhood incest. *Social Casework: The Journal of Contemporary Social Work*. Family Services *66* (7): 394–402.

This article is an account of two therapists' group work with adult survivors of sexual abuse.

Burgess, A. W., Groth, A. N., Holmstrom, L. L., & Sgroi, S. M. (1978). *Sexual assault of children and adolescents*. Lexington, MA: Lexington Books.

In a rather apolitical manner, this book addresses different aspects of childhood sexual assault, including the offender, the victim, and services.

Butler, S. (1978). *Conspiracy of silence: The trauma of incest*. San Francisco: Volcano Press.

This is a wonderful feminist analysis of child sexual abuse, including the dynamics of the incestuous family, the effects on its victims, society's response to the problem, and the role of male socialization as a cause of the prevalence of incest.

Finkelhor, D. (1979). *Sexually victimized children.* New York: Free Press.

This is a study of childhood sexual abuse, including survivors' first-hand accounts and statistics.

Gil, E. (1983). *Outgrowing the pain.* Walnut Creek, CA: Launch Press.

This is a self-help book for survivors of childhood abuse, written to the wounded child in adult survivors.

Herman, J. (1981). *Father–daughter incest.* Cambridge, MA: Harvard University Press.

This is a discussion of father–daughter incest from a feminist perspective, including a historical perspective, family roles in incestuous families, and specific treatment interventions.

Herman, J. (1983). Recognition and treatment of incestuous families. *International Journal of Family Therapy.* Human Service Press, *5* (2): 81–91.

This article examines the prevalence and psychological effects of incest, the profile of the incestuous family, the need for cooperation between mental health professionals and law-enforcement agencies, and treatment issues for the incestuous family.

Herman, J. & Schatzow, E. (1987). Recovery and verification of memories of childhood sexual trauma. *Psychoanalytic Psychology.* Lawrence Erlbaum Associates, *4* (1): 1–14.

This article reports the findings of a study of fifty-three women outpatients who participated in short-term group therapy, particularly around the issues of recovery and verification of memory.

MacFarlane, K., Waterman, J., Coverly, S., Dawn, L., Durfree, M., & Long, S. (1986). *Sexual abuse of young children.* New York: Guilford Press.

This is a series of writings on the evaluation and treatment of sexually abused children.

Miller, A. (1983). *For your own good*. New York: Farrar, Straus & Giroux.

This book examines child abuse sanctioned in the name of discipline through the use of three case studies of victims of parental domination. Two of the cases were sexually victimized as children.

Miller, A. (1984). *Thou shalt not be aware: Society's betrayal of the child*. New York: Farrar, Straus & Giroux.

This book debunks Freud's Oedipus complex, infantile sexuality, and women's fantasy/wish to have sex with their fathers and identifies the prevalence of childhood sexual abuse.

Poston, C., & Lison, K. (1989). *Reclaiming our lives: Hope for adult survivors of incest*. Boston: Little, Brown.

This book, written by an incest survivor and a therapist, describes the healing process, from finding a therapist through living in the present.

Rush, F. (1980). *The best kept secret: Sexual abuse of children*. Englewood Cliffs, NJ: Prentice Hall.

This is a feminist analysis of the sexual abuse of children, including a historical perspective, the role of the Bible and the Talmud as precursors to child sexual abuse, Freud's cover-up, and the role of patriarchy in the promotion of childhood sexual abuse.

Russell, D. (1986). *The secret trauma: Incest in the lives of girls and women*. New York: Basic Books.

This is a scholarly account of a comprehensive project on the prevalence and effects of incest.

Starzecpyzel, E. (1987). The Persephone complex. In Boston Lesbian Psychologies Collective (Eds.), *Lesbian psychologies*. Urbana, IL: University of Illinois Press.

This is an account of the effects of incest on lesbians and growing up in an incestuous family where the mother–daughter bond is damaged and the father is the principal figure in the daughter's life.

Summit, R. (1982). Beyond belief: The reluctant discovery of incest. In M. Kirkpatrick (Ed.), *Women's sexual experience: Explorations of the dark continent*. New York: Plenum Press.

In this wonderful article Summit discusses the responses of the child victim of incest: secrecy, helplessness, entrapment, delayed disclosure, and retraction. Survival skills, accommodation mechanisms, effects of incest, and treatment are discussed.

SEXUAL ABUSE BY THERAPISTS

Bates, C. M., & Brodsky, A. M. (1989). *Sex in the therapy hour: A case of professional incest*. New York: Guilford Press.

This is a first-person account of sexual abuse by a therapist, as told by an abused client and the expert witness in her malpractice suit.

Disch, E. (1989, April). Sexual abuse by psychotherapists. *Sojourner*, Cambridge, MA, 20–21.

This article points out the prevalence of sexual abuse by therapists and suggests ways clients can prevent exploitation by mental health professionals.

Walker, E., & Young, P. (1986). *A killing cure*. New York: Henry Holt.

This is a first-hand account of psychological malpractice as told by the victim of drug and sex abuse at the hands of her psychiatrist.

COMPULSIVE EATING

Hirschmann, J. R., & Munter, C. H. (1989). *Overcoming overeating: Living free in a world of food*. New York: Fawcett.

This is a wonderfully supportive self-help guide for women who have a problematic relationship to food and to their bodies.

Hirschmann, J. R. & Zaphiropoulos, L. (1990). *Solving your child's eating problems*. New York: Fawcett.

This is a revised book (formerly *Are You Hungry?*) that helps parents raise children to be free from a compulsive relationship to food and to their bodies.

Roth, G. (1984). *Breaking free from compulsive eating.* New York: Signet.

This is a supportive self-help book for compulsive eaters.

Roth, G. (1989). *Why weight?* New York: New American Library.

A follow-up to her earlier book, this gives specific exercises for breaking free from compulsive eating.

CO-DEPENDENCY

Hagan, K. (1989). Codependency and the myth of recovery. *Fugitive information.* Atlanta: Escapadia Press. Available from Escapadia Press, 454 Seminole Ave., NE #6; Atlanta, GA 30307.

This is a feminist analysis of co-dependency. Hagan asks the question, Am I co-dependent or oppressed?

Hagan, K. (1989). The wilderness of intimacy: Control and connection. *Fugitive Information.* Atlanta: Escapadia Press. Available from Escapadia Press, 454 Seminole Ave., NE #6; Atlanta, GA 30307.

This is a feminist analysis of intimacy, control, and connection. She views internalized self-hatred and oppression, which she claims are labeled "co-dependency," as blocks to intimate connections.

Norwood, R. (1985). *Women who love too much: When you keep wishing and hoping he'll change.* New York: Jeremy Tarcher.

This book explains why women replicate dysfunctional family patterns by choosing inappropriate partners and suggests ways to recover from choosing the wrong person.

FEMINIST THEORY

Dworkin, A. (1974). *Woman hating.* New York: E.P. Dutton.

This is a look at patriarchy and its oppression of women. The author examines fairy tales, pornography, and the history of violence against women. Controversial and enlightening.

Frye, M. (1983). *The politics of reality.* Freedom, CA: Crossing Press.

This is a series of feminist essays on issues that affect women.

Johnson, S. (1987). *Going out of our minds: The metaphysics of liberation.* Freedom, CA: Crossing Press.

This is a book about the evolution of feminist consciousness and the oppressions, both external and internal, that women face.

Lerner, G. (1986). *The creation of patriarchy.* New York: Oxford Press.

This is a historical perspective on the development of patriarchy and the subsequent subordination of women.

Moraga, C., and Anzaldua, G. (Eds.). (1981). *This bridge called my back: Writings by radical women of color.* New York: Kitchen Table Press.

This is an anthology of writings analyzing feminism as experienced by women of color in a racist, sexist, homophobic culture.

Smith, B. (Ed.) (1983). *Home girls: A black feminist anthology.* New York: Kitchen Table Press.

This is a series of powerful writings about the experiences of black feminists.

MISCELLANEOUS (BUT VERY IMPORTANT)

Colao, F., and Hosansky, T. (1983). *Your children should know.* New York: Harper & Row.

This book explains how we can empower children to safeguard them from sexual abuse.

Lerner, H. G. (1985). *The dance of anger.* New York: Harper & Row.

This book explains how anger has been trivialized and made toxic for women and how changing patterns of expressing anger can empower women and help them change their relationships.

Reynolds, D. K. (1987). *Water bears no scars: Japanese lifeways for personal growth.* New York: Quill.

This, like Reynolds's other books, explains the workings of Constructive Living as a means of living in the present and changing self-destructive patterns of fear and anxiety. Although in some ways it is overly simplistic and does not acknowledge the role of oppression in shaping people's lives, it can be a helpful resource.

INDEX